SPEAK AND GET RESULTS

The Complete Guide
to Speeches and Presentations
That Work in Any Business Situation

Revised and Updated

SANDY LINVER
with Jim Mengert

A FIRESIDE BOOK

New York   London   Toronto   Sydney   Tokyo   Singapore

FIRESIDE
Rockefeller Center
1230 Avenue of the Americas
New York, New York 10020

FIRESIDE and SIMON & SCHUSTER and colophons are registered trademarks of
Simon & Schuster Inc.
Designed by Richard Oriolo
Manufactured in the United States of America
10 9 8 7 6 5 4 3 2 1
10 9 8 7 6 5 4 3 2 1 (pbk.)
Library of Congress Cataloging-in-Publication Data
Linver, Sandy
    Speak and get results : the complete guide to speeches and
presentations that work in any business situation / by Sandy Linver
with Jim Mengert—Rev. and updated.
    1. Business presentations.   I. Mengert, Jim.   II. Title.
    HF5718.L56   1994
    808.5'1—dc20 93-46040
CIP
ISBN: 0-671-88996-6
0-671-89316-5 (pbk.)

THANK YOU

To my staff, who believe in the Speakeasy philosophy and whose strong support and professionalism have enabled me to do more with my business than I ever thought possible.

To my clients, whose communication needs and experiences continue to stimulate, challenge, and inspire me.

For every speaker
who feels that the connection
is worth the effort.

CONTENTS

PART II:
DEVELOP A STYLE THAT WILL WORK FOR YOU
85

PART III:
SPECIAL COMMUNICATION SITUATIONS
171

AN OVERVIEW

This is my second book on communication. My first, *Speak Easy*, focused on what I call the *spoken image*. This is more than the words we say. It's how we use the words, the sound of our voice, the way we use our bodies as we speak. Having a strong spoken image means feeling relaxed and in control before an audience. A person with a strong spoken image conveys authority and energy and demonstrates an awareness of the people to whom he is speaking. Most important, he reaches out across the invisible line separating him from the audience and works to make something happen in their encounter. Watching speakers develop that ability to get results gives me a great feeling!

But *Speak Easy* didn't treat in any detail the other side of speaking—the content. Speakers bring their spoken image—their style—to any speaking situation. But they also bring information and ideas to present. And that information or those ideas must be organized so the listeners can understand and receive them.

Most of my students are businesspeople and professionals. Their work demands that they know their content. *What* they have to say in their speeches and presentations is contained in their briefcases, law books, marketing plans, and production forecasts. So at the time I was writing my first book, I saw learning *how* to deliver a message as the biggest need for people in business and the professions. Since they had their content at their fingertips, my clients only had to develop effective styles to be able to make things happen in all their speaking situations.

But more and more, as I worked with clients on style, the organization of content in business presentations became an issue for me. Asked to watch the rehearsal of a presentation or a manuscript speech, I found it difficult not to get involved in critiquing the content. I came to realize that knowing your content—in other words, having something to say—is not the same as presenting it so that others get the message.

How can you be sure other people will receive your information? Just as speakers should reach out physically to the audience, they should also reach out intellectually to overcome barriers to their content. In content as in style, the speaker should not assume a battle line exists between her and her listeners. I realized there were things to show business speakers about making their content more effective that were just as exciting as helping them with style.

Communicating in business life is never just an intellectual exercise. Businesspeople and professionals want to make things happen. Their careers demand it, so they must be effective when they speak. The people I'm talking about have to make presentations on the progress of complex engineering projects, sell clients on expensive ad campaigns, convince the chief executive that the company must change directions to avoid financial trouble. They have to persuade reluctant distributors to sell a new product or persuade the rest of the board to make a new acquisition. The bottom line in every case is effective communication—presenting information in a way that makes things happen.

Some people are naturals at these everyday business situations. A natural inspires confidence with a relaxed, easy presence before an audience. A natural's message is clear and to the point. When a natural has finished speaking, people in the audience know what is expected of them and they do it.

The naturals I know all assure me of one thing—they don't just stand up and start talking. Their presentations are as good as the amount of time and thought they put into them. They always approach a speaking assignment or a presentation as an integral part of their job. A talk is never something to be taken lightly, a bothersome chore to be left till the last minute. Don Keough, former president of The Coca-Cola Company and one of the finest speakers I've ever heard, put it this way: "Anybody who tells you that making a speech is an easy exercise is kidding himself. When you're preparing for a speech, a tough presentation, or a negotiating session, if you're going to do it well you have to think a lot about the people who are going to be there and about what you really want to say. You can't do that by sitting down and writing notes on a piece of paper five minutes before you go in to speak."

So the naturals understand the importance of careful planning. I began to wonder about their other secrets. How are some speakers able to present information more effectively than others? How do they focus their messages clearly? How do they make their points easy to remember? How do they avoid getting bogged down in confusing facts and figures? How do they know what attitudes their audiences bring into the room? Does all this really come naturally to them or are there steps that any speaker can take to become as effective as the naturals?

The books I read on the subject were no help. They didn't have anything to do with what business executives and professionals face every day.

So I began developing a content workshop to supplement the seminars on style offered at Speakeasy. My aim was to provide the business speaker with practical tools he or she can apply in a business situation—to share the secrets of the naturals with business and professional people who can use them every day. The ideas I gathered for the content workshop have evolved into a set of simple guidelines. The result is the planning process I describe in this book; it can be easily used by any speaker, including those who have no idea where to start in planning a presentation.

I haven't forgotten about style. Your spoken image is still there every time you open your mouth. My basic philosophy about style hasn't changed, and I continue to watch clients in Speakeasy's seminars struggling to improve, taking risks, really opening themselves up in order to find a spoken image that's right for them. But I've pinpointed some new factors in developing a speaking style that can help business speakers become more effective more quickly. Discussions of the stress that speakers feel, the resistance that is present to some degree in every audience, and the techniques for handling these feelings that can help you most when you're on your feet in front of an audience—these are some of the things about style that are new in this book.

Style and content are separate issues. You can have a terrific grasp of how to arrange and present your content, but that doesn't guarantee an effective style. You can have a great style, but that doesn't mean you have something to say.

Style and content need to be approached separately, considered separately, learned separately. They form separate parts of this book. But they come together at the moment you open your mouth to speak, and they interact and influence one another. If you're shrill or visibly nervous, your well-organized content won't make much impact on your listeners. And if your style is superb but you're just rattling off disorganized details, that's not going to work either.

The really complete speaker, the natural, deals with both style and content—and excels at both. The natural brings speaker and audience together on intellectual, emotional, and physical common ground.

I want you to be a natural when you finish this book. I want you to feel in control of the total speaking situation from planning through delivery. I want you to be able to use these lessons every day to get the results you want from your communication situations. Whether you're negotiating, leading a meeting, making a speech, or presenting, and whether you have an audience of one, fifty, or a thousand, the lessons are the same. The whole process is important: each step must be done carefully if the result is to be really effective.

This book, then, is dedicated to the proposition that naturals are made, not born.

Part I

ORGANIZE YOUR CONTENT TO GET THE RESULTS YOU WANT

Introduction

In this section we look at the content of your communication—what you say when it's important to make something happen or get some result.

We'll focus mainly on presentations, the communication situation that creates the most concern for businesspeople. At Speakeasy we work with clients on all types of spoken communication—from speeches and presentations to meetings and interviews. We also help senior executives develop communication plans for their company. But the first contact people have with us is often due to their concern to be effective in their presentations.

There are some pretty obvious reasons for this. First of all, there's usually something important at stake, whether it's getting approval for a project or winning a new account. And then, the presenter has greater visibility than usual—he or she is in the spotlight and feels more exposed personally, more at risk professionally. Finally, presentations are just different enough from everyday speaking for most people to feel that special skills are necessary for success, skills they have not developed as fully as the skills they use in their business functions.

The process you'll learn in the next five chapters will help you put the spotlight where it belongs—on your listeners and what you want to accomplish with them. You'll know where to start and, even more important, where to end up. The process is a powerful tool that will make your planning more efficient and more effective.

And because our planning process is really a way to focus your thinking to get a result, you can use it for many other communication situations: a meeting, a speech, a phone call, even a performance evaluation. It also works with a wide variety of content, from financial and sales to technical and instructional. At Speakeasy, we use the process with our clients as well as for our own day-to-day communication within the company.

I believe in this process and its power to help people reach their business goals. And I know that once you've experienced its power for yourself you'll believe in it too.

CHAPTER ONE

Point X, or,
Where Do You Want to Take
Your Listeners?

Chris came to Speakeasy to work on delivering a very important presentation. President of a small computer software firm that had developed a product to help banks manage their financial systems, Chris was preparing a presentation to potential investors who could provide him the capital he needed to produce and market the product.

He had already put his content together and had come to us only to work on delivery. Because it was an unusual communication situation for him, he was concerned he might not be sufficiently comfortable and in control. During his first run-through, however, it became clear that if Chris was going to be successful with his investors, he'd need more than a comfortable style—he'd need a lot more effective content than he had prepared.

What was the problem?

Chris began his presentation with a brief history of his company and the backgrounds of the people who had developed the new software package. Then, making full use of his technology background, he described in loving—and minute—detail the major features of the software. He would certainly impress his listeners with his knowledge of the financial operations involved in banking, but after fifteen minutes of presentation, his listeners would have been asking, "So what?"

Chris was a relatively inexperienced presenter, but the mistake he made is one I continually see even among the experienced: his presentation wasn't focused on a clearly defined goal. In putting his material together he'd lost sight of what he wanted to accomplish. His content might work with a potential software customer, but it certainly wouldn't move *these* listeners closer to investing in his business. Chris had the right presentation for the wrong audience. His content didn't really answer the questions that investors would be asking.

The Most Important Question

I'm constantly amazed that people who make things happen every day in business, who are very customer- and market-focused in their thinking, switch gears completely when they have to give a presentation. Suddenly they stop trying to get results, stop thinking about their listener-customers, and start thinking about filling time. The first question they ask themselves is "What am I going to say?" They start thinking right away about the *information* and how much of it they can pass on to their listeners in the allotted time.

But that's the wrong first question. The first thing to consider is the *result* you want from the communication. Think of yourself not as a presenter who just lays out the information or recites the facts but as a *change agent*—because that's exactly what you are. As you talk, you're taking your listeners through a change process to a different place from where they started. They will have reinforced, perhaps, some attitude they have about your industry, your company, or you. They will have expanded their knowledge base or revised it. They will have made a decision or be closer to one.

They will leave more—or less—motivated to reach a goal or perform a task.

And this change is inevitable, because in a communication situation no one is merely a passive receiver. We relate what we hear to what we already know; it either fits or violates our expectations. We associate it with other things. We consider its implications for our jobs, our lives. Your primary task—and ultimate goal—as the speaker is *to direct your listeners' change so that it leads them to the result you want.*

The Presentation Journey

Think of your presentation as a journey you take your listeners on. Your listeners start at some point (A) and end up at some other point (X).

Whenever you take a trip, the first thing you want to know is where you're going, your destination, because that directs all your planning: transportation, accommodations, expenses, clothing. In our planning process, we call the *destination* of a presentation journey *Point X*. It's where you want your listeners to be when you're finished or what you want them to do as a result of your talk. It's similar to an objective, but I prefer "Point X" because "objective" is used in so many business contexts today that it's hard for people to approach it in a fresh way.

Your Point X Statement

So the starting place in planning your presentation (or any key communication) is to ask yourself, "What's my Point X?" Try to answer that question in this form:

When I'm finished speaking, my listeners will ————.

Fill in that blank with one verb, and whenever possible make that an active verb. Some examples:

. . . buy my product.
. . . ask for more information about this program.
. . . approve my recommendation.
. . . agree to a second meeting.
. . . ask for a proposal.
. . . respond more quickly when the phone rings.

Many of our clients find it quite a challenge to limit their Point X to a single active verb. But if your talk is a journey, you can have only one destination: you can't get to Chicago and Topeka at the same time. One verb—one destination—gives the clear focus you need for your planning. However difficult it may be at times to narrow down your Point X to a single verb, it's an essential discipline. If you're tough with yourself at the beginning, everything will be easier later.

I recommend an active verb because it gives you *something you can observe or measure*. You want to identify some change in behavior you can use to evaluate the success of your communication. Consider the difference between "They'll like my product" and "They'll buy my product" or between "She'll be interested in this fund" and "She'll ask for a prospectus." A listener's buying or asking gives you a much clearer measure of your success than their just liking or being interested. Even if you don't expect your listeners to take some final action, like approving your budget or contracting for your service, you are leading them to take a next step toward that final action. Try to define your Point X so that you can verify if they are in fact ready to take that step.

There's one other thing to notice about a Point X statement: *the subject of the sentence is the listener, not the speaker*. Making your listener the subject forces you to visualize them doing or being at your Point X. And if you can't really see them doing it, you know right away that your Point X isn't right.

I remember working with an account representative who was planning a presentation to the management of a convenience store chain that sold her company's products. Her first go at a Point X was "When I'm finished with my presentation, they'll agree to run this promotion." Then she imagined the president, whose stores had never run this size or kind of promotion before, agreeing; she saw the vice-president of marketing, who would have to fund the promotion out of his budget, agreeing. And suddenly that agreement didn't look so achievable. So she revised her Point X. It would have been much harder for her to use this visualizing test with herself as the subject: "I want them to run this promotion."

Sometimes you can identify your Point X for a talk right away. Other times you'll wrestle with it. Maybe you're not quite sure what result you really want. Maybe you want to accomplish so many things that you find it hard to settle on just one. Maybe you're not sure exactly who your listeners are or you see them as a group too diverse for a single destination. But whether it takes you five minutes or five days to choose your Point X, the time is well spent: this choice will drive all the other choices you make in your planning.

Check Out Your Hidden X's

One thing that makes deciding on Point X difficult is what I call *Hidden X's*. In most communication there's more than one thing you want to accomplish. It's important to identify these things so you can be sure they don't blur your focus on your primary destination, Point X.

Hidden X's fit into two categories, business and personal.

A business Hidden X is something you want to accomplish for your company. It's often a long-range destination you have for your listeners. For example, let's say you're an area sales rep for a printing company making a first call on the management of a large regional bank that currently uses another vendor for their banking forms. Your ultimate goal is to win this account, but that's far too ambitious a Point X for your first meeting. So it becomes a Hidden X. Because this Hidden X is your ultimate goal for this customer, it's important that your Point X for the first meeting be aligned with it. But equally important, your Hidden X or ultimate goal must not take your focus away from your current Point X—which in this case might be something like "They will ask for a formal proposal."

Business Hidden X's aren't all long-term. Suppose you're a financial planner speaking at a breakfast meeting of a local business association. Your business Hidden X for that talk would almost certainly be that the audience become interested in your services. After all, you're giving the talk not just to help the program chairperson out but to get exposure for you and your firm. But this business Hidden X is not your Point X for the talk—which might be something like "When I'm finished my listeners will be able to decide if a personal financial plan makes sense for them."

Personal Hidden X's

The other category of Hidden X's is personal. These are usually ego-related. As human beings, we all have egos, which sometimes feel pretty good and sometimes feel a little shaky. We have personal needs that we bring into most if not all of our communication situations.

One of those needs might be to prove something—that we're knowledgeable on this subject, that we've worked hard on this project, that we're more qualified than the competition. Sometimes we want our listeners to like us or to see us as a leader or top-notch salesperson.

Maybe your last three sales calls weren't successful. You always felt you were really good at sales; suddenly you're not so sure. So it's important that this next call be a positive experience. You've got to get the order this time to reassure yourself you've still got the right stuff.

Maybe you're going into a meeting and someone there gave you a hard time when you last talked to the group. You're really not looking forward to being mistreated by that guy again. So the one thing you most want to accomplish is to show that guy you're not a pushover.

Most Hidden X's, both business and personal, are just the result of normal human beings trying to get approval and be successful. There isn't anything automatically wrong about any of them. But they can become a problem when they get in the way of your Point X—when, without your realizing it, it seems more important to accomplish your Hidden X than your Point X.

Remember that financial planner who wanted to gain clients for the firm? If that had become his focus when talking to the business association, his presentation could easily have turned into a marketing pitch. The listeners would have left without their needs being met or their questions answered—and they would actually be less likely to be interested in the speaker's services.

If showing your listeners what an expert you are is too important to you, your presentation might include more information and detail than they need to know or can absorb. You might even complicate the subject to demonstrate your mastery of it. When this happens, you significantly decrease your chances of getting your listeners to Point X: you've put up too many roadblocks or taken too many digressions on the journey.

If making the sale this time is too important to you, you might push too hard. Or by proving you're not a pushover, you might come across as too hostile for people to feel comfortable working with you.

I'll always remember the woman in one of my style seminars who worked for a company that supplied research information to banks. Diane's presentation was taken over by both a business and a personal Hidden X. At first glance there was nothing especially complicated about her presentation or her Point X: when she was finished, her banker-listeners would have the information they needed to make decisions about long-range capital investments. But Diane never reached her Point X.

A few months before Diane's big presentation, the two top people in her company had left for other jobs. Both men had excellent reputations in the field, and the company feared that their absence would hurt business. So Diane's Hidden X was to convince her listeners that the company was as good as ever. Under the circumstances, this was a perfectly understandable, even inevitable, business Hidden X, but it became so important that it shifted the whole focus of her presentation. Instead of putting her information in a form her listeners could use, she concentrated on describing her firm's research methodology and on proving the accuracy of their data. She focused on the *how* of the study rather than the *what*.

As if that wasn't bad enough, Diane also had a personal Hidden X for that presentation. She was in line to replace one of the two men who had left, and her success in this presentation would significantly impact her chance for promotion. This Hidden X only encouraged her to concentrate even more on the detail of the methodology, to prove that she was an expert in the intricacies of what her company did.

Diane's presentation was not a success. Her Hidden X's, both personal and business, got in the way of her Point X. Within a few months she had left the company.

The point of this example is not that you shouldn't have Hidden X's. You will. You're human, you want personal recognition, and you want your company to succeed. The trouble starts when your Hidden X's get out of control. That's why it's important, while you're defining Point X, to think about your Hidden X's as well. Do some simple self-analysis and try to be as open-minded as possible when you're looking at yourself. Write your Hidden X's down.

The goal of all this self-examination is to ensure that your Hidden X's don't take over your presentation and divert your choices about content toward a different destination.

Working with clients over the years, I have found that most Hidden X's get reached if the speaker focuses not on them but on Point X. For example, if your listeners agree to purchase a service contract at the end of your presentation, they probably see you as a credible, professional person and your company as an organization capable of meeting their needs. But if, taken over by a business Hidden X, you focus your presentation on impressing your listeners with your company's capabilities, you may leave them unconvinced of the fit between their needs and your services or of your ability even to see their needs.

Summing Up

The first and most important step in planning a presentation or any important communication is to determine your Point X. This is where you want your listeners to be or what you want them to do as a result of what you say. Define that X in a single sentence with an active verb, from the viewpoint of your listener: "When I'm finished speaking, my listeners will ————." Try to pick an X that you can measure.

Then ask yourself what else you want to accomplish—what else is at stake for you and your company in this presentation. Identify those Hidden X's, both business and personal, so that you control them instead of their controlling you.

This first stage is the most important of all your planning because, once you've identified your Point X, it becomes your guide for all the other key decisions you make in putting your presentation together. If you don't have a Point X, or if you don't have the right one, everything else you do will be less effective.

It may be of some relief, however, to know that you don't have to be completely sure of your Point X at this stage in your planning. Give it your best shot and then move on to the next step.

CHAPTER TWO

Revising Point X, or, Can Your Listeners Get There from Here?

Ann was the area sales representative for a medical supplies manufacturer, and she was really excited about an important presentation to the management of a group of hospitals. She was going to tell them about a new product that reduced the risk of infection for physicians and health-care workers—a surgical glove twice as resistant to puncture as the glove they currently used.

Ann had samples of the new glove: she had results from clinical studies; she had testimonials. Within a few minutes of our work together, she had a Point X for the presentation: when she was finished talking to the management, they would agree to switch to her product.

Ann was so confident of her product's superiority and so excited about its benefits that she selected this Point X without hesitation. This isn't unusual; the first go at an X typically reflects what the speaker wants to happen—it expresses his or her desires. But since the presentation is a journey you're taking other people on, you need to check your destination against your listeners' reality. Can they get there from here?

Having a Point X for a talk is good; having a realistic Point X is even better. Are you sure that the X you've chosen is achievable? How do you know?

Identify Your Assumptions—and Verify Them

So step two in the planning process is making sure your Point X is achievable. That means taking a hard look at the assumptions behind the Point X you selected in step one.

Every time you select an X for a communication situation you are not only expressing what you want; you are also making assumptions about your listeners and the starting place for their communication journey—assumptions about their knowledge of your subject, their attitudes and opinions, their situation. *Reaching your X depends on the accuracy of your assumptions.*

Let's go back to Ann, the surgical glove salesperson. What did her Point X assume about her listeners' starting place?

> That she was talking to the people who could make a decision.
> That those people were in a "decision mode."
> That this hospital group was financially able to pay the cost difference for her new glove (about ten percent higher than the glove they were using).
> That reducing the risk of infection was a high priority for them even if it cost more.
> That they saw her company as a reputable, reliable vendor.

If any one of those assumptions was wrong, Ann would not reach her Point X, and this important sales opportunity might slip away.

As I questioned Ann about those assumptions, it turned out that one was wrong and another very doubtful. One of the key decision makers would not be at the presentation, and the management was in the process of a significant debt restructuring. Holding down costs was a high priority at that time. The cost of the new glove would be a bigger issue than Ann anticipated. After we examined her assumptions, she selected a more modest Point X for her presentation: "When I'm finished, my listeners will agree to consider a trial use of the new glove in one of their hospitals."

So your first questions in this second stage of your planning are "What assumptions about my listeners does reaching my Point X depend on?" and "Are these assumptions true?"

We've all been embarrassed from time to time, both in business and social situations, because we made some wrong assumptions—perhaps an assumption about a person's function, based on his or her title, or about the kind of business a company was actually in, perhaps an assumption about someone's readiness to negotiate or their unwillingness to participate.

Verifying your assumptions for an important communication situation is essential; reaching your Point X depends on them. So take as little as possible for granted and don't be reluctant to pick up the phone and ask a contact person or a colleague to confirm a key assumption.

People are very open and receptive whenever I ask them for information about a group I will be working with or speaking to. People like to be asked about themselves—what they want or need, what's going on with them. Rather than make you look ignorant, your questions make them feel important. One caution, however: when someone gives you information about colleagues, clients, or association members, be aware that his or her perspective is limited, too. Don't accept everything as true. (That's why I always try to get input from several members of the group, either by phone or through a questionnaire.)

How Far Away Is Your Destination?

After you've verified your assumptions, determine *how much change you expect your listeners to make to reach your Point X*—in their knowledge, in their situation, in their attitudes, opinions, or values. Now that you know where they're starting, you can figure out how long or how difficult a journey your Point X will ask your listeners to take.

Remember that I described a speaker as a change agent: when you communicate with others you are asking them to change. Most people are willing to change, to take the journey, but there are limits to how much they are willing or able to change during a single communication situation.

We can learn something about these limits from experts in persuasion: advertisers and marketers. Manufacturers don't just throw products on the shelf without testing the market; advertising agencies don't run ad campaigns without knowing their target audiences. They do market analyses to determine the levels of awareness and the kinds of attitudes their markets have toward a specific product, as well as the ways that product might be promoted. This enables them to base their campaigns on very specific (and accurate) assumptions about their markets.

If consumers have no knowledge of a product, the manufacturer or marketer must try to create both awareness and interest. Liquid soap, for example, had been used commercially for some time but never marketed for home use. Consumers first had to be made aware that liquid soap was a product they could use; they next had to be moved through other stages to the point of being ready to buy it for use at home. When automatic tellers first came to the banking industry, billboards, newspaper ads, and radio and TV spots created an initial tinge of curiosity—a need for more information—that was satisfied when the machines were installed. Similar approaches were used for introducing personal computers and cellular phones to the marketplace.

Advertisers understand that persuading people has to be done in stages. They're very clear on their ultimate destination—purchase of their client's product—but they are also clear that you can't always "get there from here." Some journeys are simply too long for one ad or one campaign.

Your presentations are no different. The Point X you finally select must be achievable in relation to what your listeners know, their attitudes, and their values. So what do your assumptions tell you about that?

What Do Your Listeners Know?

What are you assuming about your listeners' knowledge level? As they start their journey, what do they know about the idea, problem, project, product or service you're talking about?

Are they UNAWARE of it or, worse, misinformed about it?

Are they at some stage of AWARENESS? For example, do they already have some idea of this new budget process or of problems in production?

If they're aware, do they UNDERSTAND—why the new budget process, for example, is being implemented and what's different about it, or the relationship between the production problems and the scheduled shipping date for the new product?

If they understand, do they BELIEVE—that, say, the budget process will help the company allocate resources more efficiently or help them manage better? Or that sticking to the shipping schedule is important for maintaining customer relations or for meeting their sales goals?

Finally, if they believe, are they ready to ACT? Are they ready to approve or implement the new budget process? Are they ready to endorse a solution to the production problems or assign someone to develop one?

Most of us naturally go through these stages before we take action. Usually, the more important the issue, the more careful we are to go through each one. The point here is not simply that we come to an action through stages but that we typically move through only a couple of those stages at one time. So what your verified assumptions tell you about the knowledge level of your listeners—their starting place for the presentation journey—is critical. If your listeners have only just become aware of your idea and your Point X expects them to take some ultimate action, you may be asking for too much change at one time. You may need to rethink your Point X.

Think of these stages as a continuum and try to locate your listeners on it in relation to your Point X.

Making It Easier—or Harder—to Reach X

You should not only consider how much your listeners know about your subject when you reevaluate your Point X. You should also look at their attitudes and values, both toward your subject and toward you, and the circumstances in their company or industry right now. Getting to your Point X depends on assumptions about these areas too, and they can also significantly affect how much change your listeners can make or how far they will move during a single communication.

Sometimes an urgency in the current situation moves people more quickly toward an action. If a delay in shipping a new product would result in default on a bank loan, the decision maker would not wait to learn all the causes of the production problem or appoint a committee to study it. He would move all the way from being unaware of the problem to action, perhaps authorizing the appropriate supervisor to "fix it," no matter what the causes or the solution.

Is your Point X consistent with a value or attitude your listeners now have, or will it require them to change? An X that is aligned with your listeners' beliefs and opinions is more quickly reached than one requiring a shift of mind-set or attitude. Indeed, some Point X's can never be reached; they assume a change that a listener simply will not make.

Let's consider a situation where your listeners' attitudes leave them more open to change. They may have a strongly held value that will provide extra momentum for them to move farther on the journey than the typical listener. Suppose, for example, you're speaking to the management of a company whose mission is "Serving customers with a Passion." You propose a reorganization of the customer service department that will eliminate duplication in functions and make the department more responsive to customers. If your listeners are truly committed to serving customers, that commitment will incline them to move through more stages in one presentation.

Values can also keep people from making change or moving beyond a certain stage in that knowledge continuum. Suppose you are speaking to a local teachers' union about improving public education. Your preferred solution is to increase competition for the education dollar by providing indirect subsidies to private schools. Your listeners are aware of the problems in public schools and may understand the need for change, even the value of competition. But they would stop there. Because of their philosophical commitment to—and their job dependency on—public education, they would not believe in the solution you propose. If your destination is that the teachers support your proposal, you have set yourself an impossible goal. In fact, by trying to reach it with this group you will almost certainly increase resistance and create hostility. Instead, a more modest X would offer the possibility of success: that the teachers better understand why there is so much support for creating choices in education.

Consider also what your Point X assumes about your listeners' attitude toward you. Your personal credibility is an influencing factor. Say you are in marketing research and for the past two years have supplied a Caribbean island nation with information that has helped it develop a thriving tourist trade. You've given the island's officials four presentations in two years, and your recommendations have worked well for them. You now have great credibility as you go into your next presentation. Even if your suggestions represent a new or different direction, your listeners will be more open to change than if their previous experience with you had been less positive or if this were their first exposure to you.

The most common problem I've seen over many years is speakers' inflated expectations of how much their listeners can absorb and how far they can move in one communication situation. We tend to assume our listeners are as interested in or as committed to our subject as we are or that they see it from the same perspective we do. Examining the assumptions behind Point X forces us to get out of ourselves and focus on the situation of our listeners, on their reality—what they know, what they value, what's happening for them right now. Only by doing this can we be sure that the Point X we've chosen is achievable.

Of course, you can never be one hundred percent sure of your Point X because you can never completely know your listeners. But by going through this process you significantly increase the chance that you've got the best X for your communication situation. Equally important, by making yourself fully aware of your assumptions about your listeners, you'll be more likely during the presentation itself to recognize if a key assumption is wrong. A question or a comment, even a facial expression, will alert you that your listeners don't know as much as you thought they did or that they're more excited by your idea than you expected. Then you'll be able to revise your Point X on the spot.

Summing Up

By the end of this second step of the planning process you have either revised or confirmed your Point X. Let's review how you did that.

First you used your original destination or Point X to identify the assumptions you made about your listeners—assumptions about how much they know, their current situation, their attitudes toward you and your company or idea. These assumptions, taken together, define the starting point (A) of your listeners' journey.

Then you verified those assumptions, perhaps by talking to a contact person at the company or to a colleague in your own firm.

Now, with a clearer sense of where your listeners are actually starting from, you measured the distance between that Point A and your Point X to determine how much change you were expecting from them. You used the knowledge continuum, from UNAWARE to ACTION, to help you measure.

Then you examined the impact of other areas on your listeners' willingness or ability to travel that distance:

Your listeners' current situation (special pressures, politics, industry issues).

Their values and attitudes about your subject, your company, or profession.

Your degree of credibility with the listeners.

Using these categories, you were able to determine if the distance between your original Point X and your listeners' starting point was too much or too little.

Finally, you either confirmed your original Point X or revised it. You now have the confidence that the destination of your communication journey is one that your listeners can reasonably reach. Whether they'll *want* to take that journey is another question altogether, and we deal with that in step three.

CHAPTER THREE

The Message, or,
Getting Your Listeners
to Point X

You now have a destination for your communication journey—a Point X that, after examining your assumptions about your listeners, you believe is achievable. You know where you want your listeners to go and you think they can get there.

But what about them? Do they want to go? Do they want to be at your Point X?

Your listeners will have to expend energy to take the journey to your Point X. Unless they have an incentive to reach X, unless it's somehow in their interest as well as yours to be there, they won't take the journey.

So, early in your presentation, you want to give your listeners that incentive. You want to say something to them that will *arouse their interest and motivate them to listen*. We call that your *Message*.

The Message performs two crucial functions in your planning process:

It targets your listeners' journey on Point X.
It helps you to select the content of your talk.

The Message: Energy for the Journey

Simply defined, your Message is a one-sentence statement that will motivate your listeners to do the action of your Point X. For example, you are the human resources director speaking to your senior management. Your Point X is that they agree to set up a company day-care center. As you plan your talk, you look for a Message that will motivate your listeners to do this: what do they have to believe before they will agree to set up a center? The answer—and your Message—is "A day-care center will increase the productivity of our current female employees and make us more competitive for the best new hires."

As you can see from this example, you develop your Message by looking at your Point X from the perspective of your listeners. Ask yourself, "Why should they want to do that action or change their behavior in that way?" There are other ways of asking this same question:

What's in it for them?
What benefit would they get from being at Point X?
What question are they coming with that Point X is the answer to?
What problem of theirs would being at Point X solve?

The answer is your Message. In selecting a Message you'll use the information you developed when you examined your assumptions about your listeners.

Let's look at some more examples of a Message.

You're the senior vice president of a large company and, together with the CFO, you're making a presentation to the executive committee. Both your chairman and CEO sit on that committee. Your Point X for the presentation is permission by the committee to begin negotiations to acquire another company. In planning your part of the presentation, you looked for a Message that would motivate the committee to give that permission. You considered all the benefits of the acquisition and asked yourself which one would be most likely to hook the committee, which one would tap most deeply into the energy of the people listening. The Message you chose was the benefit most directly aligned with the strategic direction of the company: "By acquiring ABC Company, we will double our market share in a major target category."

Because this Message is consistent with the direction the committee is already going in, they are likely to believe the Message and do your Point X.

Suppose you're the advertising director for a TV station in a midsize market. After a couple of phone conversations, you're having your first face-to-face meeting with the account executive of an advertising firm. Her responsibility is to place advertising in this market for a consumer product company. Your X for the meeting is clear (to you and to her!): that the account executive agree to place some of her client's advertising with your station.

So you know your destination. What statement might motivate your listener to get there? Well, you know it's important for her to get results for her client; that's why her firm was hired. So you decide to use the Message: "Advertising on WXYZ will give your client the best return on their advertising dollar." You believe this Message will get the account executive's attention because it is consistent with her own goals. And if she believes the Message, she will almost certainly place the advertising with your station—in other words, do your Point X.

As you can see from these examples, you try to choose a Message that taps into the interests and values—the *energy*—of your listeners. When they hear that Message early in your talk, it energizes them to listen to you. The purpose of the rest of your talk is to get your listeners to believe your Message by the time you finish. Your aim in the content is to prove the validity of your Message statement. If you do this, you will have taken your listeners to Point X.

Distinguishing Your Message from Your Point X

It's important to be able to distinguish a Message statement from a Point X statement. Simply put, your Point X is a statement of *what you want*; your Message is a statement of *why your listeners should want it*.

Point X expresses your desire and comes from your perspective; it's where you want your listeners to be or what you want them to do when you're finished speaking. But if your Message is going to work, it has to come from your listeners' perspective—their desire, their need. It taps into their energy and focuses that energy on your Point X. The best way to get comfortable with this distinction is to look at some examples.

Point X: The office manager will agree to a demonstration of our new postage meter. (This is what you want to happen.)
Message: Our postage meter is more than a machine; it's a cost management tool. (This is why the manager will want to see it.)

Point X: The partners will agree to a new profits distribution arrangement. (This is what you want to happen.)
Message: This new arrangement will give us the flexibility we need to deal with the new economic realities in our profession. (This is why the listeners will want to agree.)

Point X: The managers will implement the new performance appraisal process. (This is what you want.)
Message: This new process will focus your employees' growth on what will make them more productive in their jobs. (This is why the managers will want to implement the process.)

In each of these cases, the Message has been selected on the assumption (verified) that it expresses something of value or importance to the listeners: the office manager wants to control and manage costs; the partners accept the importance of flexibility to their survival as a firm; the managers want their employees to be more productive. When you select a Message, be careful you don't simply state why you think they *ought* to do Point X. The Message won't motivate them if it's your reason, not theirs.

I'm often asked, as I work with clients on speeches and presentations, if the speaker should actually state his or her Point X. There's no absolute answer. In many situations your listeners will already know your Point X (on a sales call, for example). In others, announcing it may create resistance. But as a general rule it's not usually very motivating to hear a speaker tell you what she wants you to do or what he wants to accomplish. Many listeners would shrug and ask, "So what? What's in it for me?" In other words, they're asking for a Message. They may or may not know the "win" in it for you, but they have to know the "win" in it for them. So you always state your Message. Later in this chapter and in the next I'll get more specific about exactly where in the flow of your talk you state the Message to your listeners.

Same Point X—Different Messages

Because your Message is tailored as much as possible to the specific needs and values of your listeners, your Message will have to change as your audiences change. This will often be true of your Point X, too. But there are situations where similarity among the different groups allows you to keep the same Point X, even while your Message changes. In other words, different Messages can target on the same Point X. Let's look at a couple of examples.

You're the regional sales manager for a manufacturer of prefabricated housing, and you're going to be speaking to three different groups:

1. A group responsible for solving a critical housing shortage in their community as a result of a devastating hurricane.

2. Owners of undeveloped real estate looking for quick rental income.
3. Officials from a third-world country in charge of a nation-wide rural development program.

For each of these groups you have the same Point X: when you're finished, your listeners will sign a contract for a specified number of your housing units. But because the groups are different, with different priorities, you will send each one a different Message.

1. To the group responsible for alleviating the sudden housing shortage: "We can help relieve the trauma of this experience by putting people back into homes quickly and inexpensively."
2. To the real estate owners looking for rental income: "Our housing can put rental checks in your pocket within sixty days."
3. To the third-world-country officials: "Our units are sturdy enough to withstand transport over difficult roads—and simple enough to be easily assembled by local labor."

In each case your Message is appealing to the major energy source in each group—to help these people quickly, to generate income soon, to make development decisions compatible with existing infrastructure and workforce skills. Each group, hearing this Message, should be motivated to listen to your presentation; and if, at the end, they believe your Message, they will probably do the action of your Point X. The Messages are different because the groups are different, but they all target on the same Point X.

Randall, a salesman with a major soft-drink company, came to me to prepare two important presentations aimed at selling his company's diet drink to restaurant chains. In other words, he had the same Point X for both presentations. But his first presentation was to executives of a new chain that was trying to build customer traffic. The other was to a long-established restaurant group with relatively flat volume growth in their markets; the concern of this second group was to put more money on the bottom line by making operations more efficient and squeezing more profit out of their volume.

For his presentation to the first group, Randall chose a Message that stressed his brand's ability to bring more customers into the restaurants: "Consumers prefer our brand almost two-to-one over our major competitor's." Since the goal of his listeners was to build traffic and loyalty to this new restaurant, they were immediately hooked by his Message.

To the second group, managing a mature restaurant chain, Randall sent a different Message: "Our brand puts more dollars on your bottom line."

As you can see, Randall's different Messages targeted on the same Point X. The Messages had to be different because the primary need of each group was different. By tailoring his Message, Randall drastically improved his chances of getting the results he wanted.

The Message Raises Questions

I hope you now have a clear sense of how the Message functions to target your listeners on Point X. But it has another function: *the Message helps you select the content of your talk.* I indicated this in a general way when I said your content must convince your listeners of the validity of your Message. So once you've decided on your Message, you know you should include in your presentation whatever will move your audience to believe and accept the Message.

There's a very specific and easy way to use your Message to choose the content of your presentation. *Every good Message will automatically raise questions in the listeners' minds.* These are usually the obvious ones like

WHAT?—asking for an explanation or definition

WHY?—asking for the reasons why a statement is true

HOW?—asking for the process or a description of the steps that lead to the result.

Let's go back to some of the Messages we've already looked at.

"Advertising on WXYZ will give your client the best return on their advertising dollar." Someone hearing this Message automatically asks, "Why? What is the speaker basing this conclusion on?"

"This new process will focus your employees' growth on what will make them more productive in their jobs." This Message raises the questions "How does it do that?" and "Why will it make them more productive?"

"By acquiring ABC Company, we will double our market share in a major target category." Listeners will ask, "What category?" and "Why will it double our share?"

You can see that there's nothing complicated or difficult about deciding what questions a Message will raise. It's pretty automatic—and that's exactly what you want. You want a high degree of confidence that your listeners will think of those very questions when they hear your Message, because your *answers* to those questions are the content of your presentation.

You answer each question by one or more statements, each of which is itself a mini-Message—a statement that raises another question in your listener's minds. The flow of your presentation, then, is *a series of answers to questions you have raised in your listeners' minds,* starting with your Message.

Let's see how this works. Remember your Message as the advertising director to the PR account executive: "WXYZ will give your client the best return on their advertising dollar." The question raised was "Why?" Here are your answers, and the body of your presentation:

Answer #1: Because "the demographics of our viewing audience exactly fit the ideal consumer profile for your client's product."

This answer, a mini-Message, raises the questions "What are the demographics?" "Why do they fit?" After you've answered these, you're ready to move on to the second Answer to your main Message.

Answer #2: Because "our pricing structure is the most competitive in the market."

This answer, another mini-Message, raises the questions: "What is that structure?" "What makes it the most competitive?"

So once you've selected your Message, deciding what content to include in your talk is much easier. Just answer the questions! And it's not only easier to choose your content; the content you choose will work more effectively for your listeners because their involvement drives it. Their questions move it forward toward Point X.

Your presentation unfolds, then, not as a lot of information, or a series of points in no particular order, or ideas that you want to share with your listeners, but as the answers to questions in their minds, questions whose answers they want to know because your Message hooked them.

Common Problems with Messages

We work with people at Speakeasy to prepare them for many different kinds of communication situations. Often we see drafts already developed by clients themselves or by their support people.

Clients also ask us to review talks they have already given, to maximize the learning from their communication situations. While every speaker is a unique individual and every talk a unique event, we see some of the same problems with content organization over and over again. There are three in particular that relate to the Message.

Problem #1: No Message

Many speakers state their objective (a form of Point X) rather than a Message. I couldn't count the number of talks I've seen that begin with phrases like "I'd like to share with you some of my thoughts about . . . ," "It's important that you understand . . . ," or "I want to share with you some research that will be of special interest to all of us."

Statements like these are less effective than a Message because they keep the focus on what the *speaker* wants or intends. There is no real reaching out to the *listeners*, no attempt to give them an incentive to listen. The implied assumption on the speaker's part is that all he or she need do is orient the listeners toward the talk—"tell them what you're going to tell them." Sometimes such an approach will create resistance: listeners may resent being told what is of interest or importance to them. At the very least, this approach represents a missed opportunity for the speaker to use a Message to make listeners into active participants as the talk unfolds.

Problem #2: Too Many Messages

If one Message is good, then multiple Messages must be better, right?

No! When a speaker has more than one Message, that usually means he or she couldn't decide what was most important to the listeners or wasn't willing to take the risk of trusting only one Message. I am convinced that a presentation with one major Message is more effective. It keeps you focused clearly on Point X and controls any tendency to overload the talk with detail. It's more "energy efficient" in what you ask from your listeners: they don't have to go back and start a whole new train of answers to their questions.

If you find yourself wanting to use more than one Message, explore the possibility that some of them can be those mini-Messages you saw on the above outline of the advertising director's talk. See if they can be reworked as the answers to the questions a main Message raises. In this way you can still use many of the points you want to make, but with a more compelling flow.

Problem #3: The Message Comes Last

A very common feature of talks I've reviewed is that they have a Message but the listeners don't hear it until the end. This is because the end seems to the speaker to be the logical place to put the Message. After you've described the situation, defined the problem, outlined the features, or established your capability, then your listeners will be more ready to hear and believe your Message: that this approach will solve their problem, that these features provide a desperately needed benefit, that your firm is uniquely qualified to partner them in this venture.

Putting the Message last fits the logic of the speaker, not the listener. It reproduces the thinking process you went through to arrive at your Message. But your listeners want an incentive to listen at the beginning of your talk. Withholding your Message until the end may seem safer and more sensible, but you're denying yourself the resource of your listeners' energetic involvement in your talk. They may quit listening before the end and never really get your Message.

Summing Up

Another example will demonstrate the two key functions of the Message—to target on your Point X and, by raising questions, to help you select your content.

The speaker is the president of a real estate investment company addressing a group of institutional investors. Over most of the company's eight years in business, the investors have profited substantially both in the rate of return and the appreciation of the portfolio. But the last two years have been especially tough on real estate values, and the investors are nervous.

> *Point X:* "When I'm finished, the investors will continue to invest in our company." This is where he wants them to be, the action or behavior he wants to result from his talk.
>
> *Message:* "The performance you've experienced with us hasn't just been the result of a good economy and a favorable tax structure; it's been the result of our unique portfolio strategy and intensive asset management." This Message targets on X: if his listeners believe it at the end, they will be likely to continue investing in his company. The Message also directs his content selection, because it automatically raises questions: "What is the strategy?" "What do you mean by intensive asset management?"
>
> *Answer to Question #1:* "Our portfolio strategy focuses on investments with unusual characteristics." This answer raises its own questions: "What are those characteristics?" "What makes them unusual?" The president will answer these questions next.
>
> *Answer to Question #2:* "Our asset management actually adds value to the portfolio." This answer, itself a mini-Message, raises the questions: "What do you mean by asset manage-

ment?" "How does it add value?" He'll answer these questions next, using examples where appropriate.

I hope you're beginning to see how it all fits together and how critical a role your Message plays in planning a talk that gets results. But we're not finished yet. We have the body of a talk, developed out of the Message. But although you send your Message early, it's not necessarily the first thing you say to your listeners; they might not be ready to hear it. And what do you do after you've answered all the questions raised by your Message?

What you say before your Message is your Opening; what you say after all the questions are answered is your Close. We need those two key pieces before we can fit it all together.

CHAPTER FOUR

Openings and Closings

You've spent a lot of time thinking about a Message for your presentation because you understand how important that Message is to your success: your listeners' interest in it energizes them to participate in your presentation; their belief in it, by the end, will lead them to do your Point X.

So it's critical that your listeners hear your Message when you say it. That's where your *Opening* comes in. It's got a very specific job: *to get your listeners as ready as possible to really hear your Message*.

Opening Up Your Listeners

When you begin to plan the Opening for your talk, don't think of *what* but of *how*—not what content you will use to begin your talk but how you can make your listeners most ready to receive your Message. Think in terms of *function*: your opening must quite literally open your listeners up as much as possible to the Message you're about to send. It's got to clear the channels of static—misconceptions, hostility, incomprehension, forgetfulness, boredom, or fatigue—so that your listeners hear the Message loud and clear.

Make your Opening as long or as short as it needs to be to perform this function. It can be one sentence . . . or the bulk of your talk. It can be a joke, an anecdote, or a question; it can be a personal statement or a slide. The possibilities are endless, but the criterion for choosing among them is what will be most effective in preparing this particular group for the Message you've selected.

A Basic Approach

Most effective Openings begin by making contact with the listeners' current reality—their Point A or starting place for their journey to Point X. (You defined that Point A when you examined and verified your assumptions.) After all, you can't open people up unless you make contact with them, and you can't make contact with them unless you know where they are. That's Point A.

I'd like to focus first on a basic approach to developing an Opening and making that contact with Point A. I like it because it's simple and flexible, as I hope the examples will show.

1. *Tell them something they already know.* If you tell them something new in the Opening, especially at the very beginning, you run the risk that they will focus on absorbing this information—relating it to other information they have, pursuing the implications of it—and won't be fully attentive when your Message comes. Instead, try to focus them on the aspect of their current situation that will get their minds on track for your Message. In other words, you can begin your Opening by defining or feeding back to them their own Point A or starting point.

2. *Don't say anything controversial.* While there are some speaking situations where you might deliberately choose to open with a startling or provocative statement, most business

presentations should avoid controversial Openings. If new information can send your listeners off into their heads and make them miss your Message, controversial statements can send them into their emotions and produce the same effect.

3. *Construct some turn or climax to set up your Message.* If your Opening begins by defining, in a noncontroversial way, your listeners' current reality, it should also identify something incomplete or imperfect in that reality. Otherwise they have no incentive to change, to move from their A toward your X. Maybe they have a problem that's getting in the way of accomplishing a goal. Maybe they're missing some information that would make their jobs easier or more successful. Maybe they just haven't heard the end of the story. As your Opening develops, it identifies the gap or complication in their current situation—and then your Message tells them how to close it or solve it.

Three Examples of This Basic Approach

Let's look at three different Openings. Each one uses the approach I've described above, but in a different way.

Example 1

You are a veterinarian working for a pet-food company, and you're speaking to a convention of professional cat breeders. Your Point X is that they feed your company's food to their cats and kittens. The Message you've chosen is "The healthiest food for cats is food that includes animal protein." (Yours is the only company that makes such food.) The Opening you've chosen goes something like this:

You are people who do more than profit from cats. You really care about them. You've devoted your professional careers to breeding cats and you enjoy both the good feeling and the profit that come from breeding the best—the healthiest and the best-looking. And you try to do your best to breed the best.

To this point, you're recreating, in a flattering way, your listeners' current reality. Now you're going to complicate it by identifying a problem they have in reaching that "best kitten" goal:

And that means feeding them the best food. But for a long time no one was really sure what that meant. There wasn't much hard, reliable research about what really is the best diet for kittens and cats.

Now you've stated a problem, and you're ready to finish your Opening by identifying the solution, your Message:

Well, that's no longer the case. We now know what keeps cats healthy, to live longer and breed stronger. [*Message:*] The healthiest food is food that includes animal protein.

Example 2

You're the VP of marketing and you're talking to your staff after the failure of a recent big promotion. The concept was terrific, but some aspects of the execution caused serious problems. The company barely avoided a public relations disaster. Your staff feels bad about it, and liberal amounts of blame have been passed around during the last couple of months. You feel it's time to put a period to the episode and rally the troops. Most of all you want to be sure everyone has learned something from the disaster. You've identified the most important learning, and it's your Message: "We've got to get operations involved sooner in our promotion planning." You open your meeting this way:

We've all been disappointed in the failure of our "Go for Broke" promotion—and all of us, including me, have taken a lot of heat for it. We ought to. We wasted precious time and money, and we used up some of the goodwill the public feels toward this company.

This beginning of the Opening reviews your listeners' current reality. It's not a pleasant one but it's honest. On the other hand, precisely because it's not pleasant, you know they're ready to move from it. That's what you'll help them do with your *turn*:

But we've still got a job to do and other promotions to develop. So the most important thing for us right now is to figure out what we can learn from this failure. How can we use this negative experience in a positive way?

You've opened up their bleak current reality by inviting them to look at it from a different perspective. You'll define that perspective with your Message:

Well, I believe there is some very valuable learning in this experience, very valuable and very clear. [*Message:*] And that is that we've got to get operations involved sooner in our promotion planning.

Example 3

As the head of a special project team, you're preparing a report to the executive committee. Almost six months ago the committee charged you to review one of their consumer food products to find a way of getting more profit from it. You were given permission to put the team together and look at the product from beginning to end, from ingredients to distribution. Your team has done that and developed a recommendation (your Message) for the committee. You open your report this way:

Six months ago you gave me the charge to put together a team with a mission: to find some way to get more profit out of our Wonder Bar.

Here, reviewing current reality is actually a form of reminding the committee of the past. You're getting their minds back on track for your project. (After all, it's six months later, and the committee has had many other things to occupy their attention during the interval. Don't count on their remembering your project.) Continue your Opening by filling in the time since the original charge; bring them up to the present. This may seem like new information, but it actually represents a confirmation that you did what they told you to do; so it's reassuring, not distracting:

I put together a team, including [name the major players]. During the last six months we've looked at Wonder Bar from every conceivable angle, from ingredients to manufacturing to packaging to marketing and distribution.

Now you're ready to complicate the situation, ready for the turn. To this point, you've reminded them of what they once knew and confirmed what they would have expected. Now the turn is simply the announcement that really new information (your Message) is coming. All this activity did indeed produce a result:

We've looked at all our options and come to unanimous agreement that there's only one way we can get any significant additional profit out of this product. [Message:] One small ingredient change will increase our profits by three percent, with no noticeable change in taste.

There are so many types of communication situations, so many varieties of the current situation, and so many different Messages to set up that it's impossible to give you an all-purpose formula for the Opening. But I hope these examples give you a clearer sense of how a good Opening performs its function of setting up the Message. In each case, by the end of the Opening, the listeners are almost asking for the Message. Just as the Message raises questions in their minds, a good Opening often creates a question that the Message will itself answer.

Variations on the Basic Approach

The basic approach I've described above is very useful and, as you can see, allows for a lot of flexibility. But it's by no means the only way of opening a talk or presentation. If you keep the Opening's function in mind—to open up your listeners to receive your Message—you'll be on track no matter what you choose to open with. In fact, there are many ways of making contact with your listeners' Point A besides telling them, in a noncontroversial way, something they already know about your topic. Here are some variations on the basic approach.

1. *Saying something controversial.* Here you get your listeners' attention by deliberately being controversial. With this Opening you go right for the aspect of their Point A that's particularly sensitive.

Suppose you're speaking to a group of private insurers in the health-care industry. Your Point X is that they will agree to develop a common strategy of health care reform. You open this way:

> The only sensible solution to this nation's health-care crisis is a single-payer, government-financed program.

By appearing to advocate the position your listeners are most opposed to, you've certainly got their attention. Here's how you might continue with this Opening. First *pause* (this is important for the controversial statement to have the impact you want), then:

That's what a lot of people—including some key members of Congress, public interest groups, and even some of the media—would like the people of this country to believe. It's an appealing message with a powerful coalition behind it. We know that this one-payer, government-financed program isn't the best solution to the health-care crisis in this country. But knowing that isn't enough.

Here you've made the turn in your Opening, the "but" that complicates or opens up the current reality so that your Message can come to the rescue:

If we expect to be heard over such powerful voices, we're going to have to create a coalition of our own.

As you can see, this controversial Opening still sets up the Message; but it connects initially with the listeners' Point A in a different, more dramatic way than the basic approach.

2. *Laying your cards on the table.* You can use this Opening when your listeners have some hostility to you, your company, or your Message or have some expectation you can't meet. Here you put the focus directly on the very aspect of their Point A that will make it most difficult for them to receive your Message.

The vice-president of sales is talking to some major distributors who are very unhappy about a price increase for her company's software products. Her Point X is that the distributors will be motivated to sell those products. Here's her Opening:

I've gotten the message loud and clear over the last month that you're really unhappy with our price increase. Not a day goes by that I don't hear some reaction, either directly from you or from one of our own field people. I understand your feeling that we're squeezing your profits. And I know that what you'd most like to hear from me today is an announcement that we're rolling back our prices. I wish I could do that, but I can't.

Having acknowledged their feelings about the situation and defined the limits of what she can do about that situation, she now *turns* to what she can do:

What I am going to do—or at least try to do—is show you how we're going to be using the income from that increase.

Now the Message:

You're going to be getting it back—in the form of better, more competitive products to sell and better, more efficient support.

3. *Establishing common ground.* Sometimes your listeners see you as very different from them in background, interests, or values. Such a view can really interfere with their ability or willingness to hear your Message, so it's important that your Opening establish a connection with your listeners and enhance your credibility as messenger.

The president of a chemical company is addressing a local environmental group. His Point X is that they give a fair hearing to his company's proposed new plant in the area. He realizes, however, that he's initially dealing with an us-against-them attitude, so he uses his Opening to establish common ground with his listeners:

I'm not here today as the president of a chemical company or as the spokesperson for the chemical industry. I'm here as the father of two little girls, as the owner of a home in this neighborhood, and as a taxpayer in this community. In other words, I come to you today as someone who has as great a stake as you have in the quality of life in this area, now and in the years to come. And I would not be proposing a new plant here if I thought it would have a negative impact on that quality. In fact, I believe the plant will make a significant contribution to our community, and I hope you'll give me the opportunity to tell you why.

You may have noticed that this Opening doesn't have a turn in it, because the whole Opening basically functions that way: it turns the listeners' current reality around until they see the speaker in a different way, more as one of them. It emphasizes what speaker and listeners share. Once that's done, they should be ready to hear the Message, which in the example above comes in the last sentence ("In fact, I believe . . .").

4. *An anecdote or story.* There are also times when the best way to open up your listeners to your Message is through a story. You can do that when there isn't anything about their Point A that you need to address—nothing serious or significant getting in the way of their hearing your Message. They're not hostile or confused or forgetful or distracted; they just need to have their attention focused and their interest raised. A story is a great way to do that.

Television news programs have made us all familiar with the power of a story as opposed to a dry statistic or an abstract concept. Rather than merely report the rise in unemployment, the news will feature a particular family that is representative of recently unemployed Americans. This makes the statistics more real by adding emotional depth and human interest.

Another time a story or anecdote makes a good Opening is when there's nothing about your listeners' Point A that you want to address. Perhaps the group is very diverse in background, positions, or knowledge. Perhaps you want to deal with real or potential resistance in an indirect way. A story takes your listeners out of themselves and creates an alternative Point A for them. It has the power to do this because the human appeal of a story is virtually universal.

Suppose you're a customer service manager and you've been getting an increasing number of complaints about the way your department handles customer problems and requests. An anecdote or illustration could be a very effective way of opening a talk to your service reps—taking them through one customer's frustrating experience. Through the story you help them experience their own behavior from the customer's perspective—and perhaps avoid the defensiveness a direct approach would almost certainly produce.

There Aren't Any Rules

I hope all these examples have convinced you that there aren't any rules for an Opening. The basic approach should be a helpful guideline, along with the four variations I've discussed. But there are many more possibilities. In the next chapter, for example, you'll see how a speaker used visual aids as an effective Opening.

The key thing when you think about an Opening is to be flexible, because your listeners' Point A will be different with every communication situation and there will be many possible ways of making contact with that Point A. So at least initially, relax and be creative. Try to develop a couple of Openings for each presentation and then select the one that feels right to you. Just remember: you've got to open your listeners up to your Message. Anything that does that qualifies as an Opening.

Closings: X Marks the Spot

Closings usually don't provide the opportunity for creativity that Openings do, but they're no less important.

You've answered all the questions your Message raised. You've done all you can to prove your Message—to support your recommendation, to explain your conclusion, to demonstrate the feasibility of your idea or the desirability of your service. Do your listeners believe your Message now? Have they accepted it? If they have, they should be at your Point X. You targeted your Message that way.

The *Close*, like the Opening, has a specific function: *to confirm that your listeners are in fact at Point X*, that they've heard and believed your Message. There are basically two types of Close, depending on how much action your Point X statement involves.

The Direct Close: When X Is an Action

1. *Ask for a decision or commitment* to a specific action from your listeners:

agreement to a follow-up meeting to look at specific options
an order for your product
a contribution to the campaign
patience with the new system until you get all the bugs out

2. Sometimes there is no clear, single action to call for. In these cases you will *suggest or define a possible action* to consolidate your listeners' awareness or understanding and position them for the next stage if there is one:

"Tomorrow, count the number of times you turn on the water faucet and you'll have some awareness of the magnitude of our water conservation challenge."
"The next time a service representative doesn't answer your question or solve your problem, I want you to call me directly. I'll personally make sure you get what you need."

The Indirect Close

There are certain situations where the call to action or the request for commitment won't work as a Close. In those situations the best Close is usually a repeat or revision of your Message.

1. Use an indirect close when it's either *inappropriate or unnecessary to ask for the specific action* of your X:

> "I hope you can see from these examples that no one is more successful than we are at getting results for our clients in this type of negotiation." (It's obvious that you want them to hire your firm, but for this group, perhaps because of cultural or national differences, it would be inappropriate for you actually to ask to be hired.)

> "So your safety in the plant doesn't depend on understanding procedures and having the right equipment—it really depends on your attitude." (This action or behavior you want is obvious: your listeners will observe all safety procedures. It would be overkill for you to close with a call for that kind of action.)

2. Use an indirect close when there is *no real action dimension* of your Point X—when your destination focuses more on creating a feeling or motivation rather than producing an action. For example, perhaps you wanted your listeners to feel good about the job they've done or about the team they're on. In these cases close with some form of your Message.

A Note on Summary Closings

Many people like to close by "telling them what you've told them"—that is, with a summary of the key points made in the presentation. This is not a particularly effective way to end, because it doesn't target on any X. It can be useful, however, as a *lead-in to your Close,* reminding your listeners of the key answers to the questions raised by your Message. Use your judgment here. Sometimes this summary can come across as obvious or condescending; at other times it can be an effective way to reinforce your key points and signal that you're wrapping up.

Questions and Answers

Questions from listeners are a very common part of presentation situations. With larger audiences there is often a "Q&A" session that follows the presentation; in smaller groups you may be interrupted by questions from your listeners at any point during your presentation. Whether the questions come during or after your presentation, your success in reaching your Point X may be significantly affected by how you answer them.

Being successful in the Q&A situation starts with your attitude. Some speakers resent questions that interrupt the perfectly organized flow of their presentation; others feel exposed or vulnerable when control seems to pass from them to a listener: After all, you never know what someone is going to ask.

One of the major advantages of the planning process outlined in this book is that it forces you to think of your presentation as a series of questions in your listeners' minds—questions raised by a Message that is itself based on their interests and values. Because your planning has been listener-focused from the beginning, and has attempted to anticipate their questions, you should be more prepared for their questions during or after the presentation. You'll see those questions as simply part of their journey to Point X.

This planning process also gives you a framework for evaluating particular questions: As long as you have your Point X clearly in mind, you can determine which questions represent side trips and which are truly part of the journey. Your reaction to an interruption should be determined by your Point X. You certainly have the right to ask the audience to hold their questions to the end—particularly when the group is large or time is tight. If you're planning later in the presentation to cover the point you're being asked about, you can ask the listener to bear with you until the point has been explained and then ask a question if he needs more information. If the question would lead you into a genuine digression, you can acknowledge the interesting aspect of it but invite the listener to discuss it with you one-on-one after the presentation.

Sometimes a question during a presentation will cause you to significantly alter your content in order to reach your Point X more effectively. This may mean, for example, changing the order of some parts of your presentation because you sense that a particular point has a higher priority for your listeners than you had given it. Or it may mean throwing away part of your presentation because the question has opened up a more direct route to your Point X. Changing your approach to X is simply seeing where your audience is and dealing with reality.

And a question may sometimes direct you toward an even more radical action: actually revising your Point X, which can happen if a question raises a doubt about one of your key assumptions about the group.

Suppose you set a Point X for your presentation on investment strategies based on an assumption about your audience that they understand the basics of investing, such as the difference between stocks and bonds. Then a question, five minutes or so into your presentation, causes you to wonder if that assumption was accurate. At that point *you* become the questioner, asking your audience if they are indeed familiar with the terms and concepts you've been using. If most of them aren't, then you've got to change your Point X for the presentation.

The question-and-answer session that follows a presentation can be lively and stimulating. It gives you the opportunity to deal directly with your listeners. It's often the time when you are most real, because there's no script or outline to follow. I'm always amazed at how much speakers loosen up when they move from planned remarks into questions and answers. When the first question comes, they suddenly realize that people are interested and listening to what they have to say.

It can sometimes be difficult to get the session started. I've found that, instead of asking "Do you have any questions?" it's better to ask more directly "What are your questions? What else would you like to know?" Pause is part of successfully beginning a question-and-answer session, because the first question usually comes from the person who is most uncomfortable with the silence. Not long ago, in Chicago, I opened a seminar by asking "What are your expectations from our meeting today?" My audience hadn't expected to be put in the spotlight right away, and they were slow to respond. But I waited, and someone finally spoke up.

If the pause becomes awkward as you wait for a question, there are several ways to force the issue gently. You can ask the first question yourself, introducing it with some remark like, "A question I'm often asked is . . ." Or, "People like yourselves, with an interest in marketing, would probably like to know how some companies use focus groups."

If you know an individual member of the audience, you can pick him out and ask for a question directly. Be careful, however, about pushing too hard. Your listeners don't come expecting to be dragged into the spotlight, and they have a right to resent it.

As I've said, your skill in answering questions during or after your presentation is often critical to accomplishing your objective, and the planning process you've been learning will help position you for success in this critical area. But there is a technique to answering questions effectively, and I cover that in Chapter Fourteen, "Television and the Media Interview."

CHAPTER FIVE

Visual Aids

"What visuals am I going to need?" This is often one of the first questions people ask themselves as they plan their presentations. Software programs only encourage this focus on visuals by making it so easy to develop an outline of your presentation as a series of visuals. However, it's only after you've reached the present point in this book that you should turn your attention to visuals: after you've determined your Point X, your Message, the questions raised by your Message and the answers to those questions, your Opening and your Close.

It's not that visuals aren't or can't be an important part of a presentation. It's just that they do their best if they are a truly integral part of your total planning process. In the hundreds, even thousands, of business presentations I've seen over the years, all too often the visuals weren't helping the speaker get to Point X. Instead they were in the presentation for other reasons. Here are some of them:

- "That's the way we do it at my company." Some company cultures either explicitly require or have an unstated rule that all presentations be accompanied by visuals, usually lots of them. This rule may go back to some long-gone exec-utive, yet nobody wants to risk changing it. Sometimes the very companies that are open to change in virtually every area of their business have presentation cultures that are ten or twenty years old.

- Sometimes visuals are really there to serve some Hidden X's. For example, the number of visuals is determined not by the requirements of the content but by the speaker's need to impress his listeners with how much work he put into the presentation. Perhaps the particular medium or the variety of formats used is meant to show off the speaker's mastery of the software. Or the visual representation of the informa-tion is driven by the speaker's need to impress the listeners with how complicated the subject is (or what an expert the speaker is).

- Visuals are often used as a crutch for the speaker, either in the planning or the delivery. If you haven't had time to think through your presentation, you can always put your notes and data on visuals and play "read along with me." Or you can recycle visuals you or a colleague used for a similar presentation a few months ago. Then, too, some speakers try to mask their discomfort at being in front of a group by hid-ing behind the visuals: Get them focused on something other than you and you won't be so nervous.

Visuals Do Have a Place

None of these is a good reason to use visuals in a presentation. But there are plenty of good reasons. Visual communication has been with us since the day our prehistoric ancestors first scratched images into a cave wall, and today our culture is more visually ori-ented than ever before. First films, then television, then computer games and graphics have created an appetite for and an understanding of a wide range of visual imagery. And research into learning styles has demonstrated that a large number of human beings are "visual learners"—that is, their primary or preferred mode of taking in new information is visual rather than aural.

In a presentation of any length, then, there is today almost an expectation that there will be some visual component besides just you the speaker. This is an expectation you don't always have to meet; but when you do, the challenge is to make that component truly contribute to reaching your Point X. There are many ways visuals can contribute:

- They can create excitement or stir emotion.
- They can reinforce or highlight the Message or a key point.
- They can help overcome language barriers.
- They can clarify complex information.
- They can make things seem more real.
- They can provide a focal point for interaction with your listeners.
- They can create a strong, memorable image for listeners to take away.

Where to Use a Visual Aid

Once you've picked a Message for your presentation, identified the questions it raises, and outlined your answers to those questions, you're ready to identify where you can use visual support. Look at the outline of your presentation and ask yourself what points could be made more clearly, more forcefully, or more memorably by a visual. Make a list of these proposed visuals. Then state a "visual Point X" for each visual on your list: "When my listeners see this visual they will . . ." Each visual Point X should be aligned with your Point X for the entire presentation—that is, it should be a step on your listeners' journey to that X.

You'll notice that I said "your listeners' journey." One advantage of stating a Point X for each of your visuals is that it keeps you thinking of the visuals from your audience's perspective—what they see, what they need, what will happen for them. It helps you avoid using visuals as your outline for the presentation.

After you've decided where in your presentation visuals can make a contribution, *stop*. I consistently see presentations with five or six visuals that really work and twenty or thirty more that just fill up the time in between. Don't be afraid to limit your visuals to those you really need. They'll have more impact and you'll have more time to interact with your listeners.

A division head of a sportswear-manufacturing firm came to me to rehearse a presentation on the market conditions that had made it a difficult year for his firm's line of women's sportswear. He used computer-projected visuals throughout his presentation and basically read off the screen. Most of his visuals merely served as his outline, and I recommended that he drop all but six. These six painted a graphic picture of the sales figures and trends and let him move easily into a discussion of the challenges facing the company in the coming year. Using the visuals to highlight these points helped him dramatize the challenge, but limiting the number allowed him more time to really talk to his listeners. That connection was important, because he needed to establish his personal credibility and conviction if his listeners were to leave believing in the company's prospects for the future.

What Makes a Good Visual?

Another advantage of stating a visual Point X for each visual is that it can help you choose and design the particular visual. I listed above the many functions that a visual can perform for a presentation; they can basically be summarized as two: to clarify complex information or to reinforce a key point. A visual that performs either of these functions will look like this:

1. *It communicates a single point.* You can't clarify something if the visual itself is cluttered and busy, nor can you reinforce something if your listener is unable to identify quickly what's important in the visual. If you find yourself unable to simplify a particular visual, consider using a series of visuals that build to the complex point.

2. *It represents the point as visually as possible.* For most people it's easier to take in a graphic representation of your information than a string of words. So keep the words to a minimum and whenever possible turn them into charts or graphs. Even photographs or drawings.

3. *It has a headline rather than a title.* Put the point you want your listener/viewer to get from the visual right on it in the form of a headline. Here you can use your visual Point X again. Just as you used your Point X for the presentation to select a Message, your visual Point X should point you toward a headline for the visual—which is a kind of Message. For example, if you're showing the numbers for last quarter's sales, don't title the visual "Fourth Quarter Sales"; instead, identify the point you want to make with "Fourth Quarter Sales Over Goal" or "Fourth Quarter Sales Down." In this way the words reinforce the graphics and make it easier for your listeners to figure out what they're supposed to take away from the visual.

On pages 77 and 78 are some visuals illustrating these basic design principles. The first one violates all three. From this table of numbers you don't know what point the presenter is trying to make. It isn't especially visual, and it has a title, not a headline. Each of the following two visuals (page 78) takes a point hidden in the first visual and represents that point graphically and with a headline.

Many software packages today provide help in designing visuals and in presenting information graphically. If you're in a large company, you probably have people who can support you in almost any aspect of your presentation, including producing the visuals and setting up the appropriate equipment to show them. But neither the latest software nor the most expert support person can identify the point you want to make with your visual. Unless you do that first, your visual may be a pretty picture, but it won't help you reach your Point X.

PRODUCT PURCHASES IN U.S.

PERIOD	PRODUCT A	PRODUCT B	TOTAL
Q1	283,067	125,129	408,196
Q2	585,444	250,532	835,976
Q3	933,592	312,941	1,246,533
Q4	1,020,719	420,707	1,441,426

(in millions of dollars)

Choosing Your Medium—the Pros and Cons

There are many kinds of visuals available today. The old standbys of flip chart, slide, and overhead transparency have been joined by sophisticated computer-projected graphics. You can now mix media, revise visuals on the spot, and even show virtual-reality visuals in three dimensions.

Product A Outpaces Product B

Millions of Dollars

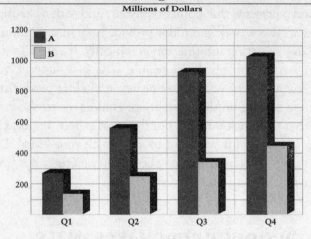

Product A Growth Slows

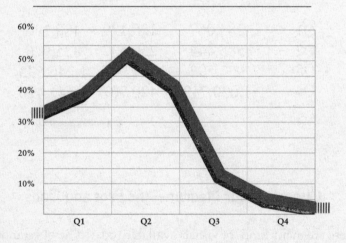

Any of these resources can make presentations more interesting and presenters more effective, as long as they're used and designed according to the basics I've outlined. When you make

your selection of media for your presentations, here are some of
the pros and cons of each type.

- **Computer projection**

Pros: +   flexibility and quick changes in production and
                  delivery
           +   "technologically current" image
           +   smooth integration of simple video, sound, ani-
                  mation
           +   wide range of professionally produced photos,
                  plug-ins, formats
Cons   −   "bells and whistles" often overused, overpowering
                  Message
           −   equipment or performance problems common
           −   clarity and brightness weak with lower-end equip-
                  ment

- **Video**

Pros   +   makes things "real" for the listener
           +   added dimensions of sound and motion engage
                  listener
           +   effective for delivering third-party endorsements
Cons   −   requires separate, dedicated equipment
           −   expensive and time-consuming to produce and/or
                  change
           −   depth of engagement for listener means strong
                  disengagement from speaker

- **Overhead Transparencies**

Pros   +   less formal than most other options
           +   flexibility for "back and forth" reference (but not
                  as easy as with computer projection); can be
                  marked on during presentation

    +   changes can be made relatively easily, almost any-where

    +   equipment available almost everywhere

    +   can be output from most presentation software packages, with wide range of professionally pro-duced photos, plug-ins, formats

Cons   –   limited projection distance

    –   relatively noisy equipment

• 35mm Slides

Pros   +   good for larger audiences because they hold image quality at large size

    +   highest level of visual quality

    +   can be output from most presentation software packages, with wide range of professionally pro-duced photos, plug-ins, formats

Cons   –   last-minute changes difficult

    –   somewhat inflexible when "back and forth" refer-ence required

    –   difficult to maintain and keep clean

• Flip Charts

Pros   +   very informal

    +   encourages interaction in small groups

    +   can be seen as an extension of the speaker (cre-ated by the speaker "in the moment")

Cons   –   cumbersome for "back and forth" reference

    –   requires stronger facilitation skills on part of speaker

• Models, Samples, Demonstrations

Pros   +   good at making things real for the listener

    +   can add novelty or surprise to a presentation

	+	can allow "physical" or tactile contact for listener
Cons	–	expensive and time-consuming to produce and/or change
	–	depth of engagement for listener means strong disengagement from speaker

You want to consider the pros and cons of each medium in terms of your Point X for the presentation and in terms of your visual Point X: What medium can best represent this point in the way I need to represent it?

But you also have to consider the logistics of the presentation situation. Do you have the time, budget, and technical support required to produce the kind and number of visuals you want? And what about the presentation site itself? How will the size of the audience, the layout of the room, the availability of equipment, affect your choice of medium?

Don't Forget the Connection

As you can see from the chart above, some media allow more interaction with the audience than others. In the next section of the book I'll be talking about the importance of connection. So I want to make the point here that you should consider in your choice of visual medium the impact it has on your ability to connect with your listeners. Don't give up "connection time" without a good reason. And here are two tips when you're using visuals that will help you maintain that connection with your listeners:

1. *Talk to the audience, not the aid.* Use the pause to check out what's on the visual and to allow the audience a few seconds to take it in for themselves. Once you start talking, focus on a human being.

2. *When you're finished with the aid, remove it or turn it off.* After your visual has made its point and you've moved on in your presentation, it becomes a distraction for your listeners. Remove it to cue the audience that you're moving on and to get them refocused on you.

Summing Up

Visuals can make a significant contribution to the effectiveness of a presentation. But visual aids are just that—*aids* to communication, signs on the journey to your Point X. They aren't a substitute for thorough planning or for the power of you. Don't block your listeners' movement toward Point X with an endless parade of irrelevant or redundant visuals, and don't turn yourself into a voice-over by giving up the advantage of a personal connection with your listeners.

My final piece of advice about visuals is to trust your own experience. You've probably seen far more presentations than you've given. What works for you as a listener? How do you feel when the presenter walks into the room with a mile-high stack of transparencies? How much attention do you pay to the presenter when the lights go down? What kinds of visuals make it easy for you to grasp the information or get the point? Pay attention to what works for you as an audience member and use that information when it's your turn to present.

You've now planned your presentation from start to finish. You know what you want to accomplish and, from your analysis of your listeners (assumptions), you have set an achievable, measurable goal (Point X). You have selected a Message that will energize your listeners to reach that goal, to do the action of your Point X. You've developed your content by answering the questions your Message will raise in your listeners' minds. You've selected an Opening that sets up your Message and a Close to confirm your success. And you've identified, designed, and produced the visuals that will help to reach Point X.

Your presentation is ready to make something happen. Your planning has positioned you for success. You've built focus, energy, and connection into the content. You've tried to make it as easy as possible for your listeners to get your message and move to Point X.

Now it's up to your delivery—your style.

You—your body from head to toe, your gestures, your voice— are a delivery system. You depend on that system to turn all your planning effort into an effective communication experience for your listeners. How you do that is the focus of the next part of this book.

Part II

DEVELOP A STYLE THAT WILL WORK FOR YOU

Introduction

Three Basic Qualities of Speaking Style

When people come to me to work on improving their style, they often tell me they want to be like other speakers they've seen who make things happen with an audience. But you don't have to become like other people in order to become a better speaker.

I've learned in teaching and working with many effective speakers that styles can be highly individual while still containing necessary and basic qualities. The people we know as natural speakers, who can make any audience sit up and listen, have unique personalities and styles. Yet they all exhibit *authority*, *energy*, and *audience awareness*—the three basic qualities of every effective speaking style. The best speakers combine these elements into styles that are confident without being arrogant, energetic without being hyper, and aware of the audience without placating it or giving up authority. The question is not how to change yourself but how to work with and improve upon who you are to put the qualities of effectiveness into your own voice and body. Let's look at the ways these qualities can be reflected in your speaking style.

Authority

An effective speaking style always contains an element of strength. I initially used the word "strength" in my teaching to mean self-esteem, but the concept has evolved to mean authority. This simply means *looking and sounding as if you mean what you say* every time you speak. Having authority in your spoken image does not mean that you are authoritarian or dictatorial or that you are cold or detached. An authoritative speaker is one whose words proceed from authority: he looks and sounds as if he knows what he's talking about. If your spoken image does not contain authority, if you don't look and sound as if you have the right to say what you're saying, your audience has reason to question your credibility.

When authority is missing in a speaker's style, it's for one of two reasons: some people never had it and aren't used to expressing it; others have it and don't use it. Many speakers simply aren't used to showing authority when they speak. Because authority is lacking in their speaking styles, these people have grown accustomed to having others dismiss their words and opinions, and this reinforces the notion that they have no authority to put into their speaking. Other speakers may have authority but leave it out of their styles because they think they'll seem too pushy or overbearing. People in positions of authority, especially men who are also physically imposing, are sometimes advised to hold back to avoid intimidating their listeners. The way to temper your authority, however, is not by suppressing it but by developing greater awareness of your audience.

Energy

Whereas authority is the impression that you have the right to say what you're saying, energy is *the impression that it matters to you.*

An energetic speaker is involved with what she is saying and sounds as if she cares about it.

It may come as a surprise, but effective speaking is hard physical work, and nothing will happen for you if you don't put physical energy into it. When you put physical effort into speaking, you look and sound as if you give a damn. Energy in your spoken image comes from your physical involvement in delivering your Message.

When you really work at making your Message come alive, you send out the impression that it's worth the investment of your energy. The audience will put only as much energy into listening as your own energy level indicates the subject is worth; you can't hold the attention of your audience for very long if you don't seem interested and involved in what you're saying. An energetic speaker gives to his speaking the amount of energy he wants his audience to give to their listening.

Audience Awareness

No business operates in a vacuum, nor should any speaker. Yet many business speakers exhibit very little audience awareness when they make presentations. I find this amazing when I consider how important the input from an audience can be. You receive a wealth of information by being aware of your audience. A raised eyebrow or furrowed forehead, for example, might signal confusion or disagreement. Signs like these let you know when it's necessary to shift, bend, or adapt your content to become more effective. They let you know when you have to work harder to get your point across. To be effective, you must see and respond to your audience, yet many speakers ignore the need for audience awareness, especially as they move from small groups to larger ones.

Speakers frequently don't allow themselves to see their audiences because they are afraid of seeing a negative reaction. But speakers who take the risk and see their audiences say the increased awareness of audience reaction makes them feel more confident, because they always know how their Messages are being received. They're no longer in the dark (a very uncomfortable feeling for most of us). Not knowing the audience reaction is more unsettling to most speakers than knowing it, even when it's negative.

Audience awareness also means that individual members of the audience feel recognized by the speaker. When you recognize your audience, they feel seen and heard. Because you've involved them, they're more likely to respond to your Message.

So audience awareness gives you information from the audience; it can make you feel better; it helps make the audience more responsive to you because you are clearly being responsive to them.

Much in the chapters that follow will focus on specific techniques to create an image that has these qualities of authority, energy, and audience awareness. But before we look at techniques or even at individual qualities, I want to emphasize the goal of these techniques and qualities; an effective spoken image. A really effective spoken image is more than the sum of its parts, more than an accumulation of techniques and qualities. It makes something happen by reaching out to the audience.

It All Adds Up to Reaching Out

When I evaluate a speaker, I don't immediately pull out a pencil and paper and start critiquing the elements of her style. My first concern is whether she is making things happen for me as a member of the audience. If I don't get pulled in, if I don't seem to want to listen, if I look around and other members of the audience are restless, I start analyzing the speaker and asking myself what techniques I would recommend to improve her effectiveness. But rote adoption of the techniques is not as important as their all coming together in a whole; if the overall effect is working, it doesn't matter if your style embraces each technique to the letter.

Following each technique rigidly would make you into a robot with no individual characteristics. The techniques in the chapters to follow are simply a base for exploration and experimentation until you feel you are projecting the qualities of authority, energy, and audience awareness. Even as you strengthen the techniques that make you a better speaker, you can retain the marks of individuality that make you unique.

I continue to be impressed by the fact that naturals, the speakers who always seem to make things happen with their audiences, combine the basic qualities we've just discussed into styles that reach out and connect. The overall effect of reaching out embodies authority, energy, and audience awareness but somehow transcends them.

An effective style reaches out by sending the speaker's energy forward to his audience. But reaching out is more than a physical quality; it is an expression of the speaker's dedication to delivering his message to the audience. How do you react when you know that someone is paying attention to you and putting effort into making a presentation work for both of you? If you're part of an audience and the speaker touches you by reaching out, you sit up and take notice. If you are the speaker, contact with the audience lets you know that they are listening. If you are convinced about the message you're delivering, reaching out relays your commitment to the audience. When you get more involved and really work to help your audience receive your message, you reveal more of yourself, and the audience can see that it matters to you.

Until you use authority, energy, and audience awareness to dissolve the barrier that exists between you and the audience, you won't ensure that something is going to happen. Reaching out is working to help the audience receive your message, working to connect with them and do whatever you have to do to make something happen. When you reach out effectively, your audience should feel that the most important thing to you at that moment is meeting them on common ground, giving up nothing of yourself but sharing an understanding. The audience should feel the depth of your commitment in a way that makes them want to match your effort to get something out of the encounter. The audience returns your commitment and involvement with their attention, and the result is an intimate feeling of sharing.

If all this sounds somewhat vague, it is because reaching out is a je ne sais quoi—an indefinable but essential quality. You know when it's there, but you can't put your finger on it. You know that a speaker has reached out to you when you forget everything else and are pulled into the speaking and listening experience.

Shedding Old Habits for a New You

Much of what you have read so far about an effective speaking style suggests psychological improvement. Words and phrases like "self-esteem," "secure," "having the right," "being willing," and "taking the risk" could suggest that your mental attitude or self-image is the key to developing an effective spoken image, and there's no doubt that one way of improving your spoken image is by working on your self-image.

But I think a poor speaker is usually just using ineffective techniques. Authority, audience awareness, and energy are expressed mainly through the speaker's use of his body and voice, so by working your body and voice as they are used in speaking, you can make your spoken image more effective, regardless of your psychological state. Working on techniques that can make you a better speaker is a matter of making choices, and you can observe and evaluate for yourself the effectiveness of each choice.

Learning to speak effectively is really no different from learning to play a sport, like tennis. First you learn the basics and then experiment with individual touches that work for you; you might choose to try a new grip to see how it affects your game. In just the same way, you can learn to make more effective choices in the use of your body and your voice in speaking.

Why don't we look at speaking the way we look at tennis or other sports—as a skill to be acquired? I think it's because speaking is something we do every day, while tennis is something we have to go out and learn with lessons and practice. We all learned to speak so long ago that the way we speak has become part of what we think of as our identity. We forget that speaking is a learned activity and think of it as an innate part of our personality.

A shy person, for example, who projects his shyness in his style, may think, "I would like to be a better speaker, but I sure can't change my personality. It's me. It's the way I am."

Such a person once asked me if she could develop a special personality to turn on like a light bulb in a public speaking situation. I asked Susan why, if she thought she could develop herself as an effective public speaker, she couldn't apply the same lessons to her everyday life. "It's not me," she said. I looked at techniques that might help Susan: she needed to move her feet apart and establish a firm base; to raise her chest, which in turn would raise her head to a level position; to learn how to breathe to support her voice; and to open her mouth wider when she spoke.

How badly you want to make lasting changes is important. Susan literally watched changes as they occurred in her during videotaping sessions at Speakeasy. Playing a role as a carnival barker, she saw that gestures she had thought outrageous were actually appropriate and authoritative. She found people would listen when her voice projection signified that what she was saying was worthwhile. She believed the changes she saw were important in her life, and she practiced and used them in her daily routine. By working on techniques, Susan quickly changed a spoken image that said, "I am shy," to one that said, "I am confident, strong, and assertive. I have authority." Susan didn't necessarily change on the inside at first, but she did on the outside.

Susan immediately got better results when she spoke. The sales presentations she made for her interior design firm became more convincing. By broadcasting her belief in herself, Susan gave an additional Message to her listeners—that what she was telling them was backed up by true authority.

What happened then? Susan was amazed at the positive feedback she received when she began using herself with more energy and authority. She soon felt more secure, more open, and more assertive than when she used herself in a closed-in way that broadcast her lack of confidence. Over a fairly short time, Susan began testing her newfound strength in other situations. She was more lively and willing to state her point of view. She saw that the shyness she thought was part of her personality was really just an accumulation of old habits that could be discarded.

When I saw Susan a year later, I barely recognized her. She was no longer "using techniques" that were foreign to her personality. I saw in Susan an everyday style which had incorporated those techniques. She had made them part of her. "You opened a door that showed me I didn't have to be locked into the same old me," she said; she was taking enormous pride and great pleasure in her "new me."

It isn't only insecure and shy people who can benefit from improved techniques in their speaking styles. David, a successful and confident lawyer in his early forties, was bright and articulate, but because he felt he had to be taken seriously by judges when he was young and beginning his practice, had become tight and controlled. He leaned back, away from his audience; he clenched his teeth; his voice droned on in a boring way. Because of the control he exerted over his body and voice, there was no energy or commitment in his body, no life in his voice. Though David had plenty of leadership potential for the political career he wanted, those qualities didn't show through.

I recommended that David work on releasing his jaw and opening his mouth to put energy into his voice and that he work on reaching out to the audience to demonstrate his commitment to what he was saying. When David saw that image of himself on videotape, he quickly decided he wanted to take ownership of the techniques that had helped him create it. A lawyer familiar with David's style in court observed later, "David is more interesting than he used to be. He doesn't seem as reined in and stiff."

Like Susan and David, anyone can choose to change techniques, and the positive effects of those choices can snowball to provide greater, long-lasting benefits. The initial, superficial change can point the way to a deep and lasting one.

Spoken Image: A Tool for Success

Speaking skills, despite their basis in techniques easily acquired and practiced, are not often ranked among other popular forms of self-improvement, and I'm not sure why. People routinely make adjustments in management style or eating habits; they jog for better health or play golf to help relax. And that's acceptable. It's OK to be a better manager, to lose weight, to be healthier, or to learn a sport. Improved speaking skills are also beneficial, both personally and professionally. But when someone says he's going to a speaking seminar, he may be greeted with the suggestion that he's going to learn to put on a phony personality reserved just for speaking to an audience. It's a common misconception that just as an actor might cover his face with makeup and put on a period costume, speakers must discard their own personalities to become someone or something different.

As you try out new techniques, they are likely at first to seem strange and unnatural. They feel "not you," and this unnatural quality is what many speakers mistake for phoniness. But as you use and practice new techniques and begin to feel more comfortable with them, the strange "not you" feeling quickly disappears.

Learning to speak well does not mean assuming a different role or character. Standing up straight instead of slouching when you address an audience, for example, doesn't make you a different person; it simply makes a better you. Learning an effective speaking style means learning to use your body and your voice as they were meant to be used.

An effective spoken image is among the many appropriate and legitimate tools to be employed in gaining success. It's like the expertise that has made you a valued financial analyst, made your economic forecasts worth listening to, made your sales and marketing skills important to your company. Your speaking skill is a business tool—one of the most powerful self-improvement techniques you can put to work in a business situation.

An effective speaking style is valuable for more than public speaking situations or business presentations. It's something you can use every day with the same positive results. The habits we adopt for public speaking work in *all* our speaking situations. Conversely, our everyday speaking style, our spoken image, carries over into public speaking; a winning style in one area is a winner in the other. People demonstrate the same weaknesses and the same strengths speaking one to one as when speaking to a group. Speakeasy's students generally see no problem with the way they speak in daily life; they take the course because they want to be better at presentations. They assume that they're effective in the ordinary situations because they're comfortable. They are often amazed to discover that the problems they thought existed only in public speaking are present to some degree in all their speaking situations. Just being comfortable doesn't make you effective. But when you have developed a spoken image that reflects the best of what you are, that style makes you effective whether you are talking on the telephone, speaking with a friend or business colleague, presenting to a small group, or delivering a speech to a full auditorium. As you think about the role speaking plays throughout your life, your goal should be a spoken image that makes you not only comfortable but effective.

Everything you read in this section on style will help you develop yourself as an effective communicator. It takes work to become the kind of speaker people call a natural. It takes work to develop any skill, and speaking is just that—a skill. A person born with natural physical prowess does not grow to become a gifted athlete without working to develop finely tuned skills. A child who can draw does not become an artist without practice and refinement. Raw talent never blossoms into skill unless it is nurtured and developed. In speaking, as in athletics and in art, we need to develop natural raw material into skills.

The Choice Is Yours

Effective speaking is a matter of making choices in the way you appear and the way you use your voice and body. You can choose to change old habits. You can open a door to the realization that you weren't born shy or afraid to speak out. As you read this part, you will see that people respond to the information you give out about yourself. The vicious circle begins when a shy person, thinking no one can possibly be interested in what he says, sends out a Message that fulfills his expectation—that what he's saying is not important. So no one is interested; the circle has come around in a self-fulfilling prophecy. You can break that vicious circle by making a positive change in your spoken image.

To become a better speaker, you must take ownership of new techniques in the same way you would commit to tennis lessons, a personal program of diet and exercise, or a new system of cost management at your office. Taking ownership of new techniques means recognizing and admitting their benefits and making them your own. The focus is on you. You are the only one you can change; yours is the only attitude you can control. This part is aimed at giving you understanding and tools that will help you feel in control of yourself every time you open your mouth.

Body builders have a saying: "No pain, no gain." Learning to be a better speaker isn't always easy, either, because it means taking a hard look at yourself and working hard to practice and develop techniques. Change can be difficult, but it can also be fun and immensely rewarding. I watch students at Speakeasy work to make a breakthrough until they're exhausted. When that breakthrough happens, it's the moment when everything comes together—when the speaker knows she has reached out and connected with her audience, when she knows she has the power to make something happen. My goal is for you to experience that breakthrough for yourself and with it the joy better speaking can bring!

CHAPTER SIX

Speaking Without Fear

The popularity of health and exercise clubs testifies to our increased understanding of the value of physical exercise and its relation to good health. Many businesspeople today run, swim, or play a racquet sport. They understand that physical activity helps them relax by releasing tension built up during a normal business day.

Most people consider speaking an intellectual exercise with no physical connection. But the demands of speaking cause a physical reaction, which you must learn to expect and control. When you're about to speak, your mind is occupied with your presentation, its content, what you plan to say. So when you feel stress starting to affect your body, you're unsure how to handle it. You can't wait until the lunch hour or the end of the day to dispel your nervous energy with exercise. You don't know how to get rid of the tension, and you feel suddenly out of control.

A simple understanding of the body's stress reaction and an on-the-spot method for controlling it can help you become a more efficient speaker.

My goal in this chapter is to help you understand that in any speaking situation you can make your body's responses work for you, not against you. Once you understand that you will always have a physical reaction to demanding situations, you can take steps to make that reaction manageable.

You can make that reaction manageable in two ways: by reconsidering what you need from the speaking situation and by using relaxation techniques. You set yourself up to receive an overload of nervous energy if you see speaking as a battle that you have to win or if you place impossible demands on yourself to be perfect. Forming more realistic goals from a speaking situation can control the nervousness you feel by controlling your expectations. You can also control your reaction by specific relaxation techniques— not just at the end of the day but when the physical reaction occurs. Training yourself to breathe and relax turns the destructive quality of tension into the constructive quality of energy— one of the basic qualities of an effective spoken image.

Reconsidering what you need from the speaking situation is an intellectual process; relaxation techniques are a physical process for a physical reaction. Both are necessary for gaining control in all your speaking situations.

Stress and Your Body

Bookstore shelves practically overflow with volumes on stress reduction. If you have done any reading about stress reduction and relaxation, you probably are aware of the fight-or-flight syndrome. Our nervous systems are equipped to help us get through tough situations. From prehistoric times, when life was a struggle for survival against wild animals and the elements, our bodies have had a built-in mechanism to respond to physical challenges. The adrenal glands release the hormone adrenaline into the bloodstream. This hormone increases the heartbeat, raises the blood pressure, and sometimes causes us to perspire. It may also create a sense of anxiety or confrontation. This surge of adrena-line puts us in a state of readiness, giving us a temporary source of extra energy to deal with the challenge. It helps us either to run away faster than we could without this additional energy or to stay and fight it out with added strength. Heroic acts—the mother's desperate effort to save her child from a fire; the hus-band's battle to remove his wife from danger in an automobile wreck—are performed by using the extra help the body gives us in these situations.

Most of us don't have that many sudden physical challenges, but we are intellectually and emotionally confronted day in and day out. A colleague criticizes our work on a proposal and our body responds as if to a challenge to fight. Being caught in traffic and cut off by another driver can cause us to pound the steering wheel in frustration to release our emotional energy. A sales clerk is unpleasant; a waiter informs you haughtily that your favorite soup is no longer on the menu; your spouse complains about the household budget; a neighbor threatens to build a fence because your dog is digging among his roses—any of these simple, everyday encounters, rationally or not, can trigger an adrenaline response.

Stress and How You View the Situation

The stress reaction can occur in any situation or activity that places demands on you to adapt. The demands may be intellec-tual, emotional, physical, or any combination. You may perceive them as threatening, challenging, or even exciting, but no matter how you view them, they will cause a physical response. This response will vary depending on the extent of the perceived demands.

Your body doesn't understand the difference between intellec-tual, emotional, and physical confrontation. It releases extra adrenaline whenever your brain signals a demand. You might be sitting outside your boss's office or a client's office getting ready for a presentation when all of a sudden you feel your gut tightening up. You think, "Boy, I didn't think I was nervous." Intellectually, you're not necessarily nervous or scared, but somewhere inside you, you feel a response that is universal in a speaking situation—you are getting ready for a battle, a battle with yourself to be perfect or a battle with another person to win him to your position.

When your body thinks you are getting ready for a battle, it will juice up with adrenaline to ready you for action. The way you see each speaking situation will affect the size or extent of your body's physical response. Sometimes we expect too much of ourselves. We want, in our own way, to be John F. Kennedy inspiring a nation to greatness or Jay Leno rattling off jokes with perfect timing. We're afraid we'll make fools of ourselves by looking odd or saying something silly; we don't want to be laughed at. We think that our audiences expect perfection in our presentations, so we end up trying too hard and controlling ourselves too tightly. The first lesson for dealing with stress is to not expect the impossible of ourselves. Remember, perfection is not what makes a speaker effective.

Another way we increase stress is by seeing the speaking situation as a battle. The more you feel you have to come out a winner in a win-lose situation and the more you view the situation as "me against them," the greater your nervous energy will be.

After my first book was published, I appeared on the *Today* show to talk about it with Jane Pauley. I had hosted a network television show in Canada before moving to the United States and was now successfully advising business speakers how to be strong and in control before an audience. But when it was my turn to be interviewed on *Today*, I was hyped up and my mouth was dry. I realized that my stress reaction was bigger than usual because I had made the interview a battle—I was competing with

Jane Pauley. I wanted to win, which meant she had to lose. When I realized what was wrong, I was able to relax and continue the rest of the interview without viewing it as a win-lose proposition.

You can reduce the level of physical response by the way you view the speaking situation. It's unrealistic to think you can eliminate all feeling. Speaking situations will always be demanding and ought always to be stimulating, so there will always be some degree of physical response.

But you will benefit greatly by controlling this response, because in a speaking situation the feeling of being out of control probably creates more anxiety than any other feeling. You must form realistic expectations of yourself, and you must also know how to relax in the face of a situation that causes stress.

A Technique to Help You Relax

At the end of a hard day at the office, it feels great to go home, sink into your favorite chair, put your feet up, and let go. You think, "Whew! What a day!" Your "Whew!" is really a deep sigh that releases all the pent-up tension of the day. There are any number of techniques designed to aid relaxation, but one of the most effective is to exhale and concentrate on settling your body comfortably. The goal of this technique is *energetic relaxation*, or relaxing while retaining the energy you need for the situation at hand. It's a technique that anyone can use to relax at the end of a day or use on the spur of the moment to relieve the tension of a speaking situation. I've used it for years, and my students tell me they find it effective:

1. Go through some simple movements to relieve tension in your body: stretch fully; move your arms over your head; bend your spine; roll your head gently in circles.

2. Sit down and gently close your eyes. Consciously choose to let go. Make this an active decision. Talk yourself into it; tell yourself that this is the most important thing you can possibly do for the next few minutes.

3. Now push your seat back into the chair so that you are sitting up straighter than usual. See how comfortable you can become by letting the chair support you totally. Imagine that you are going limp like a rag doll, but keep your head level. Let yourself go and sink as deeply into the chair as you can. I call this *settling in*.

4. Exhale deeply. See how deeply and completely you can let your breath out. As the air nears what seems to be the end, try to let out just a little more. This will lessen your tension tremendously. You are not trying to force or control your breath; you are letting go, releasing. You should be able to feel your rib cage dropping with each exhalation. Exhaling in this way should feel like a deep sigh. Do this several times.

5. Scan through your body to pick up points of tension, as if you were reading yourself on radar. When you detect tension or discomfort, see if you can think it away. Tell your body to go limp around the point of tension and to release it from your body. Do this until you find no more points of tension.

6. Now that your body is relaxed, your mind focused, and both are working for you together, visualize yourself just after successfully delivering a speech. Think of the audience applauding you, of individuals you respect complimenting you, of feeling good about yourself. Let yourself really feel the afterglow of a successful speech.

Practicing this exercise twice a day for a couple of weeks will make it practically routine. You will find that you can do the first four basic steps in a few seconds and apply it in any moment of stress. Do it in your car on the way to give a speech and when you're being introduced. When you stand up, take a moment to breathe, center, and settle in before you begin to speak.

This exercise points to the importance of breathing as a key to relaxation. Breathing is as fundamental to relaxation and speaking as it is to life itself.

Breathe to Gain Control

Much of the tension I see affecting the businessmen and businesswomen I work with can be dispelled by the simple act of breathing. Breathing works to reduce the nervousness that accompanies speaking because it releases your excess energy and keeps it from being blocked and held inside as tension. Learning to use the exhalation technique at the right time is a valuable lesson for any speaker.

Success-oriented people often are so caught up in meeting the unceasing demands of their jobs that they ignore the benefits that pausing to breathe can bring to them. My advice to these harried and harassed business and professional people is to always make the time in their working lives to breathe. We all need to occasionally let ourselves—our minds and bodies—relax, to release the tension that builds up in the course of a working day. If you make time to breathe, you also give yourself time to think. Unless you make a conscious effort to relax, a high-pressure job can keep you in a constant state of adrenaline-charged readiness. If you take the time to pause and breathe, you will also become a better listener; you will see and hear the other human beings with whom you are communicating. Simply taking time to breathe can improve every aspect of your ability to speak and listen—that is, your ability to communicate.

Tony's office was one floor below that of his boss. Every time his boss called him, Tony immediately dashed up the stairs to his office, arriving with a voice that shook with breathlessness from the exertion of the climb. Tony was then embarrassed by his quavering voice, which he felt signified a lack of control, and this made him more nervous, causing his confidence to go from bad to worse.

After we had worked together, Tony responded differently when his boss summoned him upstairs. He answered the calls by saying, "I'll be up in five minutes." Now, he said, "I take the elevator up to give myself time to breathe. I stop in the hall and take a couple of breaths. And that alone makes me feel different and stronger when I walk in. If I learned one thing," he added, "it was the importance of pausing and breathing."

No matter what you do, focusing on your breath makes you start to focus on and listen to yourself, to tune in to the rhythm of your body. That's what relaxation is all about: getting the body centered; letting your weight drop; exhaling to remove the vestiges of tension; having the courage to listen to your body for the information it will give you. These are the basic approaches to relaxation that every speaker can use as a quick prescription for stage fright: upon feeling nervous, breathe and exhale deeply to release tension.

Making Nervous Energy Work for You

Viewing the speaking situation realistically and then learning to relax and breathe will help you manage your reaction to stress. Then you can harness your nervous energy to work for you in the speaking situation, not against you.

The first day of a three-day seminar causes stress in me, keying me up for what's ahead. The people who signed up for it expect something significant to happen during the next three days. Their expectations create one set of demands. As a professional, I want not only to meet their demands but to do it with a high level of performance. My own expectations create a second set of demands. When I walk into the classroom on Monday morning, there are demands on my intellect to get the right Messages out to my audience. There are the emotional demands that come when people resist the instruction. (Maybe their boss required them to attend the seminar, and they start out thinking it's a waste of time.) And there are physical demands. It takes a tremendous amount of physical energy to hold the attention of a group over a three-day period.

All those demands, because I care about meeting them, cause that rush of adrenaline into my system. Even if I don't feel good or if I'm tired, my energy returns. I may feel tired again after working hours, but not while those demands are pulling a response from me. Since I understand what is happening, I'm not afraid when I feel this physical revving up or speeding up happen. In fact, I've come to welcome this surge of energy as a sign that I'm stimulated enough to do my best.

I am able to harness this surge of energy because I no longer view the seminar as a battle—and although I place great demands on myself and know that my students expect me to be a real professional, I still don't expect to be perfect. And throughout the three days, especially at particularly tense or tiring moments, I take time to breathe.

You Can Choose to Relax

Tony learned to breathe and relax once he learned what his choices were. Control in a speaking situation comes not in being controlled but in having many choices. When you try to clamp down on your body to control nervousness, you reduce the number of choices available to relieve that nervousness. So the goal of relaxation is to get the body settled and open, ready to respond when you opt for the choices that will reduce your tension and make you a more effective speaker.

Remember in approaching all your speaking assignments that there are two ways to deal effectively with the physical reaction to the speaking situation. First, reconsider your view of the situation; don't feel that you have to be perfect and don't make it into a win-lose situation for yourself. Second, use the relaxation technique at moments when you feel stress beginning to build. Then be prepared to harness your nervous energy to work for you.

Speaking is demanding, but it can also be enjoyable and fulfilling if you choose. Now that you know you don't have to feel wrung out by your nervous reaction, the chapters to follow will show you how to build upon your new confidence with the look, body image, and voice of a confident, effective speaker.

CHAPTER SEVEN

Your Visual Image

Your visual image is how you look. More than the features you were born with, your visual image is the composite picture drawn by the choices you make in putting yourself together: your personal grooming; the way you wear your hair; the material, color, style, and fit of your clothing; your glasses, if you wear them. Facial hair is an added factor in a man's visual image; makeup is part of a woman's.

What does your visual image have to do with speaking? Although visual image isn't the most important part of your spoken image, it's nevertheless the first impression your audience receives, and first impressions are hard to change. When you walk into an office or boardroom or onto a platform as a speaker, the audience first sizes you up by what they see. You want that initial evaluation to be consistent with who you are and what you want to accomplish. If it isn't, it can negatively impact every other part of your speaking situation. Just as the Opening of your presentation provides the audience with a reason to keep listening, your appearance sends out signals about you and the quality of presentation you're about to deliver. Those signals can work for or against you.

Much of what we do with our physical appearance is the result of habit rather than careful, deliberate choice. Yet people are making assumptions about us all the time on the basis of what they see—dress, hair, and grooming. If we can step back and see ourselves as others do, we can increase our awareness of what those assumptions are likely to be. With this increased awareness, we are in a better position to make choices that send out the signals about us that we want others to receive. Ultimately, of course, we can't control the assumptions people make about us; but we can make choices that are more accurately aimed at getting others to see us the way we want to be seen.

Seeing ourselves as others see us is seldom easy and sometimes even painful, because many of us have a lot invested in the way we put ourselves together. Some simple questions may help get the process started, questions that focus on the impact of your visual image on your authority and your audience awareness.

1. Do I look comfortable in my clothes?
2. Do I look like I believe I'm worth spending some time and money on?
3. Do I look like someone doing the kind of work I do? in the industry I'm in? at the level I occupy?
4. Are my visual-image choices consistent, or am I sending out mixed messages in the way I put myself together? (For example, expensive clothing that doesn't fit well; a conservative style of clothing and large, flashy jewelry.)
5. Does my visual image make me seem open and accessible to listeners, or does it put up barriers between us?
6. Is there anything about my visual image that would be distracting to a listener?

I have no interest in prescribing how you should look or what you should wear. I do, however, want you to become more aware of your visual image and able to make more conscious choices about it. And those choices will not always be the same, either over the course of your career or even when you're speaking to different audiences. But I do believe that a visual image that supports an effective spoken image is one that says, in effect, that you're comfortable with who you are and respectful of your listeners. This often means striking a balance between expressing your own individuality and adjusting to the appropriate expectations of others. Balancing authority and awareness.

Visual image is a very personal thing. All of us assume a self-image that we take quite seriously. We are easily hurt or offended when someone suggests that we need to change it.

In my seminars, people are usually open to making dramatic changes in their voices and the way they use their bodies in speaking situations. That's not the case with their hair or their clothing or their jewelry. Because visual image is the first thing we notice about people, I used to dive right in on the first day of the seminar and tell clients when they needed to improve aspects of their visual image. I was surprised when they reacted more strongly and with more resistance than to practically anything else I did or said during our time together. I soon learned that a comment like "Have you ever considered trimming your hair?" is much more likely to hit a nerve than one such as "You need more authority in your voice." Now I wait until students have had a chance to become more open to the idea before I suggest ways they might look better and more authoritative.

If you have strong feelings about your visual image, your gut may tighten up any time someone makes a comment about it— for example, that you could look more professional, or less sexy, or more "age appropriate." That strong reaction is a clue that you should pull back and think about why it's so important to hold on to that part of your appearance.

Your visual image won't stand alone once you begin speaking. Other images come into play for your listeners as soon as you start talking. The other elements of your spoken image are your body and your voice. What they convey—their authority, energy, and awareness of the audience—follows your visual image just as the body of your presentation follows your Opening.

CHAPTER EIGHT

Your Body Image

Your body can be a friend or an enemy in a speaking situation. You already know that you can make choices affecting the way you feel and your ability to relax. The choices you make about using your body when you speak are tremendously important; they can affect your sense of control and have a profound effect on the way your audience sees you. Your body can express the basic qualities of an effective spoken image—authority, energy, and audience awareness.

The first thing I do regarding body image in the Speakeasy seminar is introduce students to the balanced stance—the best way to stand in a speaking situation. I've found it best for two reasons: it projects an image of authority to your audience and it allows you to deal with your body's tension so you can feel better when you speak.

Stance: Your Home Base

The open, balanced stance is simple and comfortable, yet few people automatically stand this way when they rise to speak to a group. The elements of a balanced stance are these: feet apart, lined up more or less underneath the armpits; weight evenly distributed from side to side and from front to back, with weight on both the heels and balls of the feet; arms comfortably by the sides. Using the open, balanced stance doesn't mean you have to be frozen into it or that you never move out of it. Sometimes your legs and feet get tired from standing in one place during a long presentation and you simply need to move—which you'll see later in this chapter can be an expression of energy. But the balanced stance is your home base—it's where you start and where you return, a solid position from which strong statements can be made.

The right stance contributes to authority by allowing you to feel the security of owning your own space. It is a confident posture that makes you look authoritative without looking combative or aggressive. It simply confirms for the audience that you know what you're talking about: you have a right to be there. By allowing your body weight to settle, it lets you be more relaxed and aware of your audience.

Don't Stand for Instinct or Bad Habits

When people start to feel shaky and out of control, they instinctively go into a protective mode. Male speakers are likely to take a fighting stance, their feet wide apart, knees tightly locked, chest puffed up, and shoulders thrown back in a classic aggressive posture. The results unfortunately are anything but what they want: the locked knees add tension to the legs, causing increasing discomfort; the puffed-up chest doesn't permit proper breathing for speaking; tension across the chest and shoulders increases the feeling of nervousness. Making the wrong choices lets the effects of tension accumulate: the more you try to exert control when you feel nervous, the more you'll tighten your knees, chest, and shoulder muscles and the more out of control you'll feel. The more shaky and tense you become, the less authority you project to your audience.

Protective reactions like the fighting stance are instinctive. But it's not a physical battle you're girding up for. You don't have to lock your knees until your legs shake, because nobody is going to try to push you backward. You don't have to puff up your chest and pull your shoulders back until you can barely breathe, because you're not trying to frighten an opponent or take a swing at somebody. You can decide not to do these things. If you make the right decisions, you can continue your speech or presentation with a more relaxed body that you can control.

A woman reacting instinctively to the implied threat in a speaking situation may fall back into a posture that worked when she was younger and things weren't going her way: she crosses her legs at the ankle, folds her hands protectively in front of her, tilts her head to one side with her chin up, and smiles like the cute little girl who had her daddy wrapped around her finger.

Betty had the body image of a little girl; when she spoke, she stood with her feet close together, clasped her hands in front of her, and tilted her head. On the first afternoon of the seminar, I asked Betty to begin using the balanced stance, lining up her feet under her armpits. When she assumed the stance, I asked her how she felt.

She said, "I have to tell you that this feels uncomfortable, awkward, and masculine."

I told her not to look down at her feet and asked her to look at my stance. "Do I look awkward or masculine?" I asked.

"No," she said, "you look fine. But my feet are a lot farther apart than yours." I asked her how she knew that. "I can just tell," she said.

"Betty, look down at your feet," I replied, and she discovered that her feet were not as far apart as mine were. She was so used to standing with her feet close together that her perception was distorted. Being aware of your options can help you avoid instinctively using a posture that may increase your tension and make you look and feel precariously off balance.

People sometimes claim they feel more relaxed standing with their weight on one leg, the other knee bent and one hand in a pocket—almost the drugstore-cowboy slouch of the James Dean era that signified not giving a damn. Speakers who use this stance try to protect themselves by not seeming too involved, as if a deliberately casual posture were a way of fending off failure. This posture looks casual to the onlooker—and detracts from authority. At the same time, it actually increases tension, because one leg is tight all the way down to support the weight. The balanced stance, however, decreases tension because it distributes the weight evenly on both sides of the body. Two legs are better than one!

Charles, a hospital administrator, was a good speaker, but he leaned slightly backward when he spoke. Since he was over six feet tall, his backward lean made him look down on his audience even more than he would from a normal stance; it made him look aloof, as if he didn't want to be open and involved with his audience, and it hampered his authority by suggesting Charles was really a little scared. I told Charles he was giving up authority by leaning away from the audience and recommended he put more balance into his stance.

A stance that is too narrow makes you look insecure and placating, and this also detracts from authority. Keeping the feet too close together denies the speaker a firm base to stand on. Without a firm base, the tendency is to try to struggle harder for support or control and this again increases tension. Wearing high heels makes a narrow stance even more precarious.

Every speaker should use an open, balanced stance as a natural authoritative base for speaking. Adopting the right stance and using it routinely doesn't mean being a robot. You don't have to use your body the same as another speaker to be effective any more than you have to dress the same as other executives in order to be successful. But a balanced stance is basic to using your body in an open, relaxed way, saving energy, lessening the tension you feel, and increasing your authority by giving you a firm home base.

Gestures: A Natural Form of Expression

Natural movement expresses energy and commitment. There is nothing more naturally energetic than movement, but when movement is repressed, it reduces the commitment of the speaker and eliminates an escape valve for built-up tension.

The energy contained in children's bodies makes it hard for them to sit still. They seem always to be wriggling and squirming; their bodies and voices are freer than those of adults. When they tell a story or ask for something, their faces, their bodies, their whole beings are involved in the delivery.

As we grow up, though, we impose a lot of control on ourselves. Probably because of the countless reprimands we've received, we stop acting with the openness we had as children. Students at Speakeasy always feel silly and embarrassed in the exercise that requires them to use exaggerated gestures as they pretend to be carnival barkers or flower vendors on a street corner. But then they're amazed at how natural those gestures look when played back on videotape and how much more interesting and committed they look and sound.

I'm not suggesting you have to return to the flamboyance of childhood to put energy into your spoken image, but there is a happy medium between the uninhibited bodies of children and the controlled bodies of adults. Your goal should be an adult body that is open, balanced, and relaxed—that will work with you rather than against you, that can express your commitment. It's naturally better to let your energy out in movement by involving your body in the delivery of your message instead of working against yourself by keeping your energy bottled up inside.

Dan was a good example of someone who wouldn't let his energy out. When he stood to speak, he kept one hand on the opposite wrist, usually in about the same position where a fig leaf would be. He pressed down with the top hand while the other kept desperately trying to gesture. I suggested that Dan let his captive hand go; when he freed his hands from each other and let them fall naturally to his sides, he began to gesture in a way that expressed his energy.

Unnatural gestures can be distracting. Just as the open, balanced stance is home base for your feet, the home base for the arms is relaxed at your sides. Your arms don't naturally bend at the elbows when you stand in a relaxed way, and your hands don't naturally fall into a fig-leaf position. Almost any gesture will be effective if it is open, natural, and relaxed.

To keep your movements natural when you speak, remember that your hands, arms, shoulders, and torso are all connected; restricting movement in one area restricts it in another. Men who draw back their shoulders and puff up their chests hinder their ability to gesture as well as to breathe. They restrict their ability to move, limiting the body involvement that should go into delivering their Message. Perhaps because of the traditional military image, many men try to convey authority with an expanded chest and squared, pulled-back shoulders. In business speaking situations, however, the military image is reminiscent of a rigid tin soldier; the arms can move only in puppetlike arcs from the elbow.

Some speech advisers suggest that the only power gesture is a big gesture above the chest. Very little we say in business, or anywhere else for that matter, is so profound as to demand that kind of dramatic gesture. Moreover, people who use gestures this way never really let go of the arms. The so-called power gesture then becomes distracting, because it communicates tension. If we never drop our arms and let go, we convey the feeling we aren't settled and relaxed, that we are protecting and shielding ourselves.

The exception to this rule comes when you speak behind a lectern. If you keep your arms by your sides, you're likely to hit the lectern every time you begin to gesture. Most speakers find it comfortable and effective to rest their arms on the lectern in a loose way that leaves them relaxed but free to gesture. Don't lean with all your weight on the lectern, however.

You don't have to gesture constantly to be an effective speaker. But speakers have to let their physical energy out in order to be effective. When people begin to show their energy and commitment in speaking, they often gesture a lot. They also often find that gesturing is not the only way to express and let out energy.

The Walk

Walking can be an effective tool for releasing tension and expressing energy. When you're standing in front of an audience and feel some excess energy, you can take two or three deliberate steps to one side. It's much better to take a couple of steps than it is to stand there shifting your weight around; this contains your energy and makes you look restless.

A walking pause serves to emphasize a significant point in a presentation or punctuate a major break in its organization. Used in this way, the walk underlines a transitional statement: "That is what our plant will do to provide jobs in your community." (Move a few steps. Stop. Take a balanced stance.) "Next I'd like to talk

about the taxes we will add to your city treasury by locating here."
Talk for a while and then return to your original position.

As with any technique, overdoing it diminishes its effect. In
the case of the walk, which faces you away from the audience as
you move from side to side, overdoing it can jeopardize your rapport with the audience. The more you walk, the more casual your
presentation will be and the less committed you will appear. The
balanced, planted body has more directness and authority.

If you don't use the walk as an accent for a pause but rather talk
as you walk, the power and force of your words tend to be dis-
persed toward the walls on either side of the room. You should
always look at your audience to retain your awareness and to keep
the energy flowing between you and them instead of to the walls.
Looking at your audience during a walking pause is dramatic. It
holds the audience, but it can seem stagy and make them feel
uncomfortable if it's done too often.

I ask Speakeasy's seminar students to make walking more natural by practicing. Stand in a firm, balanced position, walk a few
feet and then return to the firm stance. I'm not suggesting you
have to walk in order to be a good speaker, and you certainly
should not diminish its effectiveness by overdoing it. But it can be
a valuable technique, an option available to you when you need
it. Gestures and walking—all movements, in fact—are not ends
in themselves but means to an end: a more energetic, committed
style.

Speaking Behind a Lectern or While Seated

How much do standing and gesturing really matter when you're
behind a lectern where people can't see your feet or your arms?
The stance is important wherever you are, whether you're
behind a lectern or beside a flip chart or screen. When you don't

have a firm stance, even if most of your body is hidden, the off-balance attitude will be reflected to your audience in your upper body and probably also in the energy you send out with your gestures. A firm base allows you to feel better and use yourself more effectively behind the lectern. And remember that if you use the walk, you won't be hidden behind the lectern all the time. By the way, if you're using a lectern with a large audience, be sure to request a neck or clip-on microphone so that you won't have to restrict your movement to accommodate a stationary one.

Many people say they do a lot of speaking in meetings across a desk or around a conference table. Certainly in one-on-one meetings or small meetings in an office you usually sit, but in a slightly larger group you have a choice. Just because other speakers have sat doesn't mean you have to. Most people can be more energetic when they're standing, so you should consider whether breaking precedent in this situation will help you reach your objective. And if people have been sitting for a long time, both you and your audience may be especially in need of the extra energy you can put into your presentation when you stand.

But if you choose to sit, all the principles of being centered, balanced, and settled and of reaching out that apply when you're on your feet apply when you're in a chair. The most common mistake people make when they're seated in a meeting is to lean back, which makes them appear uninvolved. Leaning back detracts from your speaking and your listening, because it prevents your energy from flowing to the audience. You don't perform as well, and your audience thinks you're not giving out to them.

Your body is speaking for you all the time. You may be more conscious of it if you're up in front of a group without any props in front of you. But your body can work for or against you whether you're out there by yourself, beside a flip chart, behind a lectern, or seated at a conference table. The basics still apply.

You've seen how your body can express authority and energy when you speak and make you feel better at the same time. Now you're ready to add the important quality of audience awareness.

Awareness: How to Get It, How to Use It

Focusing on your listeners is another of the choices you can make with your body that can give you one of the essential qualities of an effective speaking style and also make you feel better in a speaking situation. Focusing provides audience awareness; it is a continual source of information about your audience and their reaction to your Message. It allows you to see and benefit from the support for your Message that exists in the audience. And when you don't see support, it allows you to make intelligent adjustments to reach your Point X.

It's How You Look at Someone, Not How Long

In every speaking situation, the audience gives out subtle signs to the speaker. Looks of curiosity or confusion let you know your message isn't getting through and that you may need to adjust your content if you want to be effective. Focusing on your listeners gives you important feedback; it's your way of silently asking them, "Is what I've just said clear?" The information that comes from seeing your listeners will also affect your style as well as your content, causing you to increase your energy if you see signs of boredom or to reach out more at signs of resistance or hostility.

Really seeing your listeners doesn't mean scanning them, looking at some arbitrary point over their heads, or, if it's just one person, fixing your eyes in the distance over his left shoulder. It means looking at and seeing individuals in the audience as if each one were the only person in the room, the one person whose reaction is important to the success or failure of your presentation. It means talking to individual human beings, not to some amorphous mass called an audience, the marketing group, the Downtown Civic Club, or the executive committee of your company.

Awareness is developed in stages. The first stage is learning to look at members of the audience and not stare off over their heads. Many beginning speakers find this the hardest part, because they've never really looked at the people they're speaking to before. The second stage is learning to see the people in the audience, so that you know (for example) how they're sitting, what color their hair is, and whether they're wearing glasses. The third and final stage, which is what awareness is all about, is listening to the audience with your eyes, using this source of input to sense important developments in their mood and responses. The speaker who is listening with her eyes is aware of frowns, puzzlement, approval—the whole range of reactions, in fact, that any speaker can expect to encounter.

One of my staff members once listened to a lecture by the actor John Houseman. She said that as he went around the room taking questions, he caught her eye and held it. He had seen something in her expression that made him think she had a question. She did not, but he held her gaze long enough to make sure and then went on. This illustrates a good speaker's sensitivity to his audience.

Don't confuse seeing or focusing on your listener with eye contact. It's not a staring contest. Never distract yourself by trying to count the number of seconds of eye contact you have with individuals in the audience. Timing your seeing is truly form over substance; it may allow you to look at everyone for the same amount of time, but it prevents you from really seeing anyone. Awareness means genuinely looking at a person, taking in what you see, and responding to it as you go on. You should look directly at the person you're talking to as if you were speaking one to one.

It is also important to try to look at everybody within reason-able viewing range. There is a tendency among speakers to avoid seeing people who seem bored, skeptical, or hostile and instead to aim their entire Message at the people in the audience who look sympathetic or merely attentive. Those listeners are then saddled with the responsibility of providing feedback to the speaker for the duration of the speech or presentation. Focusing narrowly on one or two members or even half of the audience permits the energy in the rest of the room to fade away and distractions to occur.

Once I was standing at the back of a room waiting my turn to speak at a communications workshop for midlevel managers, and I saw the speaker before me concentrate all his attention on the people to his right. They were responding by leaning forward attentively and listening with considerable energy. But the people on the other side of the room were having quiet conversations, looking around, and doodling. The speaker had lost one side of the room, while just across the aisle was an attentive audience.

It's important to include as many people as possible in your see-ing. Look around the audience at random and pick people out; don't try to go row by row or take one side and then the other.

Be aware of room arrangements that can interfere with your ability to focus on your listeners. A U-shaped seating pattern in a conference room, for example, makes it easy for the speaker to ignore the people at the ends, so don't move too far into the U and leave part of your audience behind you. People on the speaker's side of a conference table can also get left out if the speaker isn't careful, because a genuine effort is required to lean forward and look up and down the row. Sometimes the speakers' platform, if there is one, is too low to easily see people toward the back of the room. A speaker who sees members of the audience leaning and craning around the people in front can help them out by occa-sionally moving away from the lectern.

Learning to See One Another

Of the many reasons we tend to avoid seeing our listeners, one may be that we are afraid of being seen by others. We translate the nervous energy that speakers feel into the fear that the audience will be bored, skeptical, or disapproving of what we say. Cameron, who found it almost impossible to look at people when he spoke, put it like this in the seminar: "I learned how hard it is for me to see you. It's hard because I'm afraid of being seen. If I see you, there's a part of me that says you'll see me. And you won't like what you see."

I'd helped many students work on developing awareness of their audience, but it wasn't until Cameron got up and talked about his fear of eye contact that I really understood how difficult it is for some people to develop this part of their speaking style. But when you begin to see the audience for the first time, you're likely to find a lot more support there than you expected. One of my students was a lawyer who was to argue an important case before his state's supreme court. Since Mitchell was an associate in line to become a partner, the case was important to his career with his law firm. Mitchell told me he was nervous when he went before the nine justices. But he said that as he began his argument, the justice who had been toughest on a lawyer in the previous case nodded and gave him a look of encouragement. He said that small gesture of reassurance made him relaxed and confident from then on. If he had not been focused on the justice long enough to see that slight sign of receptivity, he—and his case— might have suffered.

Adam was an engineer who was an adequate speaker, but his delivery lacked the extra measure of life that would have made him really good. He explained his problem as a lack of awareness: "I began to realize that during the seminar this week, I've been looking at you, but I'm not sure I was really seeing any of you. The thing I need to do is talk to you as individuals, because you're the ones that make up this whole audience that I'm talking to. As I do just that, it's amazing to me the kind of real communication I have with each of you. It really makes me feel good, and the thing I realize is that I see each of you as individuals, and this helps me to relax." Helping students experience real awareness is always a major goal for me, because once you've experienced it and seen how it can make speaking easier and not more difficult, you'll always want to do it.

Moira was articulate and capable; she said she was nervous when she spoke, but the feedback she got showed that her audience felt she was aloof and uninvolved and didn't care about them. After a presentation in which I told her to focus on each member of her audience, she sat down and said, "That's the first time I've ever seen anyone!" As she began to see people when she spoke, her aloofness fell away and she became much more level, direct, and involved with the people she was speaking to. I saw Moira a month later speaking to a group of about four hundred people. The audience no longer saw her as cool and distant but reacted positively to the new impression of involvement that she gave.

Like Adam and Moira, students tell me that once they begin to look at and really see people they feel they can be more open and honest with the audience and with themselves. Allowing yourself to show your commitment and share it with the audience has an impact on the way the audience sees you. The impression you give is that you're concerned about what you're saying, and the audience finds it easy to become involved along with you.

Authority, Energy, and Audience Awareness in Body Image

So you can stand and move and see in ways that will enhance your spoken image. But because doing these things is a natural use of your body, they also make you feel better and more in control. The open, balanced stance gives you maximum support and allows you to relax. Gestures and walking allow you to release pent-up tension. Focusing on an individual listener helps you to be comfortable because it allows you to see interest and support.

Choosing these techniques contributes significantly to an image that has authority, energy, and audience awareness; it also helps you feel more at ease and in control of yourself.

The elusive quality of reaching out can also be expressed in a speaker's body image. Leaning forward slightly from the torso has the effect of sending your energy out to the audience. Forward-directed energy from your body, face, eyes, and voice spells commitment to your audience.

Reaching out is what you would do if you were asking the location of a restroom in a country whose language you did not speak. You would not stand there with your arms folded in front of you and quietly ask for the restroom, barely opening your mouth to speak. You would reach out with all of the means of communication you had available—your facial expressions, your eyes, your mouth and voice, your body, hands, and arms. You would make a sincere, perhaps a desperate, effort to get people to understand what you wanted.

If you look from the side at an effective speaker, you will see him not just staying inside an upright, rectangular box formed by the space around him. An effective speaker leans forward, breaking the vertical plane of his own space, sending his energy in the direction of the audience and of common ground.

But as I noted earlier, the quality of reaching out transcends the techniques that make an effective body image. Neil, a speaker in one of my seminars, had a firm base and good eye contact and expressed his Message with energy. He was a big man who spoke with his hands folded comfortably in front of him. In his final talk, he reached out beautifully—he looked at people, his energy flowed forward, and he pulled in every member of his audience. When he looked at the videotape, however, Neil was disappointed in himself.

"I guess I'm your worst student, Sandy," he said. "I'm still holding my hands in front of me."

"It doesn't matter," I told him, "because in spite of that, you reached out and made something happen." Your ability to connect with the audience is the bottom line in being an effective speaker.

An effective body image does all these things and forms the second component of an effective spoken image. Your body controls your voice, which is the third component in your spoken image. Your voice, too, can project an image of authority, energy, and awareness to your audience.

CHAPTER NINE

Your Vocal Image

Most people don't realize that they can make choices in the way they use their voice. They feel that voice is something they were born with and that making changes in their voice would involve years of voice study. But you don't need to put in the amount of time an actor or a singer does to make your voice more effective. What you do need is first of all to listen to your voice objectively. Use a tape recorder and hear the impression your voice conveys to others.

The next step is to understand the way the voice works—and the five elements of voice that really can make a difference in the way you sound.

The last step is to practice, using voice exercises that will help you to develop an awareness of your voice and to hear the changes that are possible.

Most of the problems in making your voice more effective can be solved by this process of inquiry, understanding, and practice.

How Voice Works

Just what can be done with the body's normal equipment for voice production? The physiology of voice goes back to breathing. When the lungs need air, the intercostal muscles between the ribs contract and the ribs swing up and out. The diaphragm—the umbrella-shaped muscle just below the lungs that separates the chest from the abdomen—contracts, then descends and flattens, causing a slight displacement of the abdominal organs and an expansion of the upper part of the abdomen. The size of the chest cavity is increased, and air rushes in to fill the vacuum. During exhalation the muscles relax and return to a resting position, and air is forced out of the lungs.

The importance of this is twofold. First, when we inhale, the diaphragm and other muscles are in a state of contraction; when we exhale, they relax and return to a resting position. So inhalation is tensing, tightening; exhalation is relaxation, letting go. Second, the diaphragm controls the rate of exhalation, but the actual push comes from the upper abdominal muscles, sometimes called the belt muscles. So air is pushed not from the throat, chest, or lungs, but from the abdomen.

This process has everything to do with voice production, because voice is produced on exhalation. As we exhale, the push from the abdomen forces air out of the lungs through the voice box, or larynx, located in the throat. The vocal cords, or folds, inside the larynx vibrate as the air passes through, producing sound in much the same way that air vibrating a stringed instrument produces sound.

So voice is produced by a push from the gut, not from the throat. And since voice is produced on exhalation and exhalation means a physical relaxation or letting go of the muscles involved, speaking, in a very real physical sense, means letting go.

The basis of good voice production is relaxation—letting it happen the way it was intended to happen. Tension interferes with this natural process. Because voice is a function of the body, tension anywhere in the body can interfere with voice; but the most common tension points involve the muscles surrounding the speech center in the jaw, throat, and neck, as well as muscles in the shoulders, chest, and stomach.

From the above you can see that voice is produced in four steps:

1. Inhale. The inhaled breath provides energy for your voice. Tension in your speech center will limit the amount of breath you can take in and thus limit your energy.
2. Begin to speak. Breath pressure from the exhaled air does all that is necessary to make the vocal cords vibrate to produce sound. Straining or trying to push from your throat will interfere with rather than help voice production.
3. Send your voice forward toward the audience to give the voice fullness and carrying power.
4. Open your mouth and let the sound out. Tight jaws and clenched teeth distort and muffle the voice.

The four steps of voice production are interrelated, and each begins with and depends upon relaxation. Tension in your chest and stomach prevents you from breathing effectively and giving your voice a source of energy; tension in your throat strangles the sound at its source and affects the pitch of your voice; tension in the mouth and jaw is felt in the throat and also affects your ability to articulate.

Relaxed Breathing Provides Energy

Relaxation in the chest and throat and proper breathing for a source of energy are necessary to achieve an effective, energetic speaking voice. Breathing is so common to us that we hardly give it a second thought when it comes to speaking. Yet I believe that nothing is so important as the correct use of the breath. Untrained speakers tend to stop breathing effectively for speech whenever they get nervous or tense. If you don't pause and are too tense in the chest to inhale correctly, you will be able to take in only short, quick breaths. If you feel you have to keep talking no matter what, you will speak with far less air than you need.

Tension, the common, unconscious reaction of many people to the challenge of a speaking situation, is the natural enemy of a speaker's ability to breathe correctly. Rigidity, especially around the chest and abdomen, makes it nearly impossible to get a good deep breath that allows you to put energy into your speaking voice. Relaxation and pausing to inhale are the keys to breathing effectively for speaking. Fortunately, proper breathing, as seen in the relaxation exercise in Chapter 6, "Speaking Without Fear," is a key to relaxation.

We breathe normally through the nose, inhaling or exhaling about every four seconds. Breathing for speech, however, requires more air than we normally use, because we talk for longer than four seconds at a time. And it would make for an awkward presentation if we paused for four seconds every time we inhaled to replenish our breath supply. But since we exhale naturally in the act of speaking, we have to stop talking for some period of time in order to inhale. Frequent brief pauses—less than four seconds— are essential for a good pattern of breathing that will support the voice.

Trying to take in more air more quickly through the nose is noisy and looks haughty. For speech, you should breathe through the mouth. This is perfectly natural, since you must open your mouth to speak.

Many speakers, especially if they are required to use a microphone, worry that the audience can hear them breathing each time they inhale, even though they take in their breath through the mouth. It's one thing if when you inhale you sound as if you are slurping soup. But the sound of natural breathing is nothing to be concerned about. No listener expects you not to breathe, to deny yourself the energy you need to speak.

Inhaling effectively for speech should not be confused with exhaling for relaxation. When you're feeling the nervous energy that builds up before a speaking situation, that's the time to use the exhale, the letting go of the breath, to relax and settle down. But before the first word comes out of your mouth, you must fill up with breath to support your voice and give it its energy. As you continue to speak, your concern should remain with the inhale, to make sure that your voice has the support it needs.

Articulation for Energy and Authority

Articulation, the act of shaping sounds into words, gives your voice the qualities of energy and authority. It may seem obvious, but good articulation is first a matter of opening your mouth. Proper breathing is the first step in developing an effective voice, but learning to relax your jaw and open your mouth is a close second.

Well-articulated speech adds authority by sounding and looking more definite. When you articulate, you sound as if you're more involved with the words, which in fact you are—your mouth is taking an active part in shaping your message. Articulation also adds energy and commitment. Think of angry speakers you've seen. They inject vigorous meaning into their words and say them as if they mean them, with an extra measure of expression. Anger usually improves a mumbler's articulation, but you don't have to be angry to articulate.

There are two main reasons why people don't have good articulation. Some speakers have never thought about using the mouth energetically. Their words just slip out in a mumble with a listless, lackluster sound. When you use your mouth with more energy, it makes you feel more involved and in control. That active feeling sometimes gives a feeling of self-consciousness to people who aren't used to it. Other speakers, many of them top executives, subconsciously clench their teeth and jaws as an expression of control. Even though they are committed to their messages and aren't afraid to project authority, the sound doesn't come out because they don't open their mouths.

As you try consciously to open your mouth to articulate, don't be concerned that it feels foolish, flamboyant, or out of control; as with the use of gestures that at first seem exaggerated, what seems overdone and unnatural when you're not used to doing it is seen by your audience as sincere and committed. You don't have to stretch your mouth open. The simple act of opening your mouth requires relaxation; the muscles that hinge your jaw must be relaxed to let the mouth drop naturally open.

Many men seem to think precise articulation is prissy or affected. Roger was a student who had a lazy mouth—he barely opened his mouth or moved his lips as he described the advantages of advertising in the magazine he represented. Potential advertisers thought that if Roger wasn't willing to make himself understood, he must be uncommitted to the value of what he was trying to sell. In other words, they interpreted his lazy mouth as a lack of authority and commitment.

I urged Roger to stop thinking he would be seen as affected if he took the trouble to form his words properly and to realize that energetic articulation would give his voice more authority and commitment. I told him to begin shaping his words as if he were speaking to people who lip-read. He said it felt exaggerated and strange at first, but his fears vanished when he saw in a videotape how authoritative and energetic he looked as he spoke about the value of his magazine as an advertising medium. The more convinced Roger looked, the easier it was for him to convince his audience; the attitude of potential advertisers was captured in a comment by one of Roger's fellow students: "If he's sold, I'm willing to be sold, too."

One of the nicest things about making a change in one aspect of your voice is that other changes will sometimes result. This is because the components of voice production are interrelated. Once I was leading a group of women, all in real estate, through a series of exaggerated articulation exercises. I encouraged them to open their mouths wide and really form their words. They were stunned to hear their voices drop almost an octave. The jaw tension that kept their mouths closed had also caused throat tension, which gave their voices a shrill pitch. When they opened their mouths, their jaws and throats relaxed, letting their voices drop to natural, lower-pitched levels. Their relaxed, lower voices gave them all greater authority.

Downward Inflection: The Sound of Authority

You can add authority to your voice in another way, with downward inflections. Inflection is the way you vary the pitch and tone of your voice according to meaning. There are two basic types of inflection: upward and downward. Downward inflections make your words sound definite, confident, and persuasive. Most phrases and sentences should end with definite downward inflections. In other words, use your voice to put periods at the ends of sentences. Upward inflections—the tilt to a higher pitch at the end of a word or toward the end of a sentence—carry the sound and sense of a question, as if you are unsure of yourself and a little scared. They make you sound polite but tentative and not very firm, like a person asking for approval. Upward inflections compromise your authority and replace it with uncertainty, insecurity, hesitation, doubt, or surprise:

You should diversify your investments; ↗
invest in property ↗
as well as in stocks and bonds. ↗

The use of upward inflections in this example makes the speaker sound as if he's not sure of the investment advice he's giving. It would sound much more definite with the voice going down at the end of each phrase.

You should diversify your investments; ⬊
invest in property ⬊
as well as in stocks and bonds. ⬊

Hal, a free-lance investment broker, wasn't getting the results he wanted in his client presentations. He was confident with his content and asked me to listen to his presentation to see if I could spot the problem. The strongest message that came through was the uncertainty in his voice. Almost all of Hal's sentences ended with upward inflections, which were undermining the confidence of his clients in the advice he gave them. When I suggested to Hal that he concentrate on using downward inflection, he told me he wanted to avoid seeming pompous. But when he heard on his tape the uncertainty in his voice, Hal immediately understood why he was having trouble selling his services—his upward inflections were robbing his voice of authority.

When Hal began putting confidence into his voice with downward inflections, his words carried the same impression as his thoughts about his investment advice: "I feel definite about this, and it's what I believe. I'm sharing my best opinions simply and directly, and I have no reason to sound uncertain."

The Pause: Instant Authority

Violin virtuoso Isaac Stern was once asked how it was that all professional musicians could play the right notes in the right order, but some made beautiful music while others did not. He replied, "The important thing is not the notes. It's the intervals between the notes." Just as the best musicians add an extra shade of meaning—the difference between good music and great music—by spacing their notes, the best speakers know the value of pausing for effect.

The pause is an incredibly powerful technique to give your spoken image authority, energy, and audience awareness. Pauses are needed in speech to allow you to relax and breathe to give your voice energy; they give you time to see the audience, to think and gain control of your speaking situation by "getting with yourself."

The pause lends importance to the words just spoken and thus contributes to the impression of authority. It demonstrates that you are comfortable with silence and that you feel in control of the speaking situation. A common tendency among speakers is to fill the spaces that might otherwise be pauses with "ahs," "uhs," and "you knows," or by clearing the throat. This need to fill up all the blank space detracts from authority because it communicates a fear of silence.

Pausing also adds energy to speech, first because it is an opportunity to inhale and replenish the energy behind your voice. Pausing as you walk a few steps away from your centered position before the audience (a technique discussed in Chapter 8) lets you take in energy for your voice by inhaling while releasing excess energy from your body.

Pausing adds energy to speaking in still another way. Here is an example of a dramatic pause that adds energy:

"There is one thing we must do to increase our sales next year." (Pause.) As the speaker pauses the audience begins to ask, "What? What is the one thing?" An audience that is asking for your information is going to pay attention to what comes next. In fact, people will become noticeably quieter and physically more attentive as they wait for you to continue. A pause before a point you have led your audience to expect can make the air crackle with electricity. That is a silence more dramatic than words and is a good way to lead into your most important points.

Pausing also helps your sense of audience awareness, because it gives your audience time to absorb what you have said and prepare for the next point. By pausing after you make a complex point or an involved statement, you are showing consideration for your listeners' needs as well as giving yourself time to assess their reactions.

Randy, a government employee who conducted public hearings on health and safety regulations, told me that every time he spoke at a hearing he thought, "If I can just get all this out and sit down, I'll be OK. If I stop, I'll go blank." He also wanted his listeners to know he had a grasp of the regulations being proposed.

Randy's audiences, however, were not impressed with his knowledge of the regulations. By rattling them off without stopping, he didn't distinguish important points from routine ones, and he gave listeners the impression that he wanted to push the regulations through without public input. What's more, he wore his audiences out by being hyper and hard to follow, leaving them thinking, "Boy, I'm getting exhausted just listening to him. What in the world is he saying, anyway?"

I suggested to Randy that the solution to his problem was pausing consciously every so often to give himself a chance to breathe and think. Once he forced himself to pause, Randy found himself less out of breath and more in command of his material. He told me he was surprised to find that his pauses also emphasized what he was saying and gave his audiences a chance to digest the information.

As he got more used to pausing, Randy began to understand that the pauses helped the audience calm down, too. Listeners could focus on him and understand and remember what he was saying. They also began to see him as a really confident speaker and found themselves waiting for his next words or pondering the impact of what he had just said. They could pick out vital points in the regulations because Randy's pauses signaled places where he wanted to let the information sink in.

Projection and Resonance

Of course, all the authority and energy in the world won't do your voice any good if it doesn't reach the audience. The last step in making your voice its most effective is to reach out with your voice, to project. Projection is related to resonance. A voice coach might tell you to project and get more resonance in your voice by aiming the voice forward to the "mask" of your face or by thinking of throwing your voice forward to the audience. My advice is, once you've mastered the other qualities of an effective voice, try to put that voice out almost into the laps of your audience. That mental image, together with the physical effort of throwing your voice out in order to connect with the audience, teaches most people to project without the help of voice exercises.

Projecting your voice doesn't mean shouting, however; loudness alone won't get your voice out to the audience. You can reduce your volume but use your mouth energetically and think about putting your voice forward, and you will be easily understood without being loud. What is known in the theater as a stage whisper is done by removing almost all volume from the voice but using the mouth and sending the voice forward to make the words understood.

Businesspeople should remember that a voice that is too loud seems out of control; it diminishes authority and may seem abrasive. A voice that is articulated with energy and reaches forward to the audience, even with little volume, will seem much more in control.

Resonance is a quality of voice more easily explained in a class-room than in a book, and problems with resonance are more eas-ily corrected with professional help than by practicing on your own. "Resonance" means "resounding." The sound created in the larynx resounds in the chambers of the nose and mouth. This is what gives the voice its quality of fullness. A well-resonated voice has more authority and is easier to listen to. Resonance often results naturally when other qualities of the voice are practiced and achieved, as with the women who found their voices becom-ing lower and more resonant when they practiced articulation.

Many women complain that their voices don't sound serious enough and don't have enough authority. For most of them, paus-ing, breathing, and opening the mouth more and relaxing the jaw will tend to lower the voice and make it fuller. But an additional step is sometimes needed. I think it has to do with the way you feel about yourself: you have to be willing to put weight into the sound of your voice. Think about getting the voice forward and speaking forcefully rather than keeping it back up in the top of your head, which gives the quality that people describe as imma-ture. Work on the basic qualities already discussed to put author-ity into your voice and use a tape recorder to experiment with expressing anger until you hear the sound you want coming through.

People whose voices are too high and weak often try to force the tone downward, like a tenor trying to imitate a bass singer. Instead of trying to force your voice lower, it's more effective to seek out your fullest, most natural voice, which is probably lower to begin with. Projecting your voice out toward the audience will keep it from being too light and thin, which detracts from authority.

Ellen was a commodities broker who told me she had always heard her high, weak voice as an expression of femininity. But someone who had heard one of her presentations told me that her audiences thought, "Wow, what an airhead." She sounded like a little girl, and the people listening responded accordingly; they thought she didn't really know enough to be taken seriously. Ellen corrected the problem by projecting her voice forward.

Ellen understood that a fuller voice can be pleasing and that a woman can be feminine by sounding like a woman instead of a little girl. As Ellen's business audiences caught the difference in her presentations, they thought of her as having more authority and a fuller personality. Responding to her new authority, they were far more ready to receive and respond to her Message.

Some of the things that irritate people about their voice, like too much nasality, are also matters of resonance. For a better understanding of resonance and projection, turn to the resonance and projection exercise later in this chapter. Businesspeople who want quick results may also want to consider the help of a voice coach or a speech pathologist.

Other Voice-related Problems

Speakers who breathe, articulate, use downward inflection, pause, and project have the basic elements required for effective speaking. But people frequently encounter voice-related problems that interfere with their effectiveness. Speakers occasionally ask me, for example, "What should I do if I'm too loud?" If your listeners are complaining that you're too loud, I'd recommend that you have your hearing checked to see if it is a factor. It's more difficult to monitor your speaking volume than any other aspect of voice; recruiting a friend or associate to help you can give an initial indication whether you should seek the advice of a hearing specialist.

A raspy, gravelly voice is what speech pathologists call glottal fry. Businesspeople feel it as a tightness in the throat and hear it as a shaky quality that makes them sound tired and nervous.

Inadequate breath support and tension in the throat are the main causes of this problem, and sometimes the throat tension may be caused by speaking with the chin pressed in and down upon the throat. The way to deal with a raspy voice is to pause more, breathe effectively for speech, think about putting the voice forward, and open your mouth more when you speak. If a raspy voice persists after you take these steps, you should seek the advice of a professional. It could indicate a physical problem.

What About Accents?

Regional accents are a charming reminder that each of us is an individual with a background that is at least partially revealed in our speech patterns. Yet people ask me all the time if they need to get rid of their accents. I almost always say no. A regional accent is part of your personal identification, and there's no reason to deny your audience that essential identifying factor. It is one way of reaching out to the audience, giving them another means of getting to know you.

What people often identify as their accent, though, may be in fact a voicing characteristic or habit that has built up over the years. One of these is nasality, which, combined with an accent, may impress people as uncultivated. In our American culture, a nasal-sounding voice gives this impression no matter what accent it is combined with. Lily Tomlin's telephone operator Ernestine on television's *Laugh-In,* is a good example. On the other hand, a full sound projected through an open mouth will impress listeners as more refined no matter where you're from. People also tend to believe that lazy articulation is a characteristic of their accents, but this is also easily changed to let the real accent come through.

Before we look at some exercises that will help you develop the qualities necessary to an effective spoken image, let's review the basics:

Relax. Relaxation is basic to all aspects of voice production.

Inhale. Your breath is the energy source for your voice.

Articulate. Energy and authority in your voice come from good articulation.

Use downward inflection. The definite sound at the end of words and sentences gives your voice authority.

Pause. Effective pauses provide energy, authority, and an opportunity for audience awareness.

Project. Think about reaching your voice forward and handing your words to your audience.

Make Time to Practice

As you begin to make changes in your vocal image, you should try to set aside frequent times when you can listen to your voice on a quality tape recorder that does a good job of reproducing sound. It's better to practice by listening to the playback after each few minutes of speaking rather than filling up one side of a cassette before playing it back.

Practicing in this way, if you stick to it, will make you an expert analyst of your own voice. Listen for indications of whether you're breathing enough, relaxing your throat, bringing your voice forward, opening your mouth, and energizing your articulation. Listen for pauses and downward inflections. The more you practice, the more ideas you will have about how to improve what you hear.

Working on your own will let you explore the sound your voice makes. Don't deny yourself the opportunity to experiment with your voice as a means of expression. Mark out times in the day when you can carry your experiments over into normal conversation. You may decide to pause during a telephone conversation, for example, instead of saying "uh" or "you know." You can choose a moment at a cocktail party when you involve your body as you speak in order to put more energy into your voice. If you can, listen to yourself in these situations. I recommend playing back the voice mail messages you leave for others. This is a simple, hassle-free way to monitor how you're actually using your voice when you're thinking primarily about other things.

I have found that one of the best ways to practice is to read poetry out loud. Since poetry is usually written for voice, it can provide some fun and interesting challenges in the way you use your voice. It pushes you to use more energy and develop a better tone. I recently met a man who had an excellent, warm voice and was one of the better speakers I have heard among businessmen. I complimented him on his voice and he replied, "I read poetry aloud. I wonder if it's helped me." He did it because he loved poetry; he wasn't trying to develop his voice, but that was the effect.

Regardless of how you go about practicing them, the exercises that follow are designed to help you breathe and relax and to improve all aspects of your vocal image by adding energy, authority, and audience awareness. Almost all of them require the investment of considerable energy. Don't try to go only as far as you think you need to go for your particular situation. Throw caution to the winds! Go to the extremes; you'll then find it much easier to return to a happy medium that is best for you and your vocal image.

Once you begin a routine of practicing voice exercises, the results of your practice will quickly spill over into your everyday speech. In no time at all, you may develop a sixth sense that tells you each time you speak if your voice carries the authority, energy, audience awareness, and reaching out that you intend to convey. Knowing that your voice is effectively carrying your Message and working in harmony with the rest of your spoken image provides a constant source of satisfaction and a sense of achievement. The confidence that comes from knowing your vocal image is revealing you at your best reinforces your commitment to change.

Exercises to Help Your Voice

Developing Breathing Awareness

1. Sit with your body relaxed but upright and in good alignment, with your feet flat on the floor. Relax your arms and hands on the arms of your chair or in your lap. Relax your stomach muscles. Close your eyes and breathe passively. Now notice what is happening to your beltline. As you take air in, your beltline expands; as you let air out, it recedes. This rhythmic expanding and receding of the beltline is what happens during good, natural, deep breathing. If this doesn't work for you, try panting very slowly, like a dog. Now you should feel the movement at the beltline.

2. Tension interferes with this natural process of good, deep breathing. For a graphic demonstration, tighten your belt muscles as much as you can. Now take a deep breath. You can feel the difference: you are not getting as much breath as before. Thus you have little control over the outflow of breath, which produces your voice. You may also feel tension developing in your shoulders, your chest, and even your throat. Tension in these areas surrounding your speech center can interfere with the vibration of the vocal folds.

3. Now relax your stomach muscles and take quick, deep breaths through the nose. Do the same thing again, only this time inhale through the mouth. Notice that this method is much quieter. You don't have to open your mouth wide to get a good, deep breath very quickly with little or no sound at all. This is the way you should breathe for speech.

4. You do not always need to take your fullest breath to say what you want to say. But as you develop your breathing awareness, you will find that the more urgent and numerous your ideas, the more likely you will need to pause and take in a full supply of breath before you start talking. When you need time to think and choose your words carefully as you go along, you can pause frequently and take in less air.

5. When you take a deep breath, you do not have to use it all up immediately. You can pause, hold your breath by setting your waist muscles for a moment, and then continue speaking. Say "sh" and take a breath. Say "sh" seven times on one breath. Now say three medium-long "sh" sounds. Finally say "sh" as one long, sustained sound—"ssshhhhh." In each case, there is a difference in the muscular action at the waist. As you pause in producing the sound, you also pause in using the stomach muscles to push out the sound. This exercise is designed to give you a sense of how much breath you need to express thoughts of varying length.

6. Your voice runs out of energy if you do not get adequate air, and you look weaker, too. Standing in front of a full-length mirror, expel the breath from your lungs in one quick exhalation, then talk. There is enough residual air to produce voice for a short time, but notice how little power your body has as you strain to speak. Now take a deep breath, with relaxed stomach muscles and an open mouth, and talk. Notice now how much stronger your body looks and feels and how much easier it is to produce voice without straining.

Breathing and Voice Practice

1. To check the difference that breathing can make in your voice:

Tape-record yourself as you count from one to ten out loud, using your normal breathing pattern.

Now take a full breath before each number and count, trying to use up each breath on each number. After each number, blow out any leftover air and take another breath for each new number. Count to ten this way as you tape-record yourself.

Now take as much air as you need to say series of numbers of different length. Try to take only as much air as you need for each series as you say "one, two," "one, two, three," "one, two, three, four," and so on, until you count to ten, again recording your voice.

The latter two examples should sound stronger than the first, since you are taking in more air. The second exercise, in which you breathe for each count, is tiring, since you are wasting air. The last exercise should feel just right, since you were able to anticipate the amount of air you needed each time.

2. Each of the following lines is longer than the one before it. Take enough breath to say each line:

I pause to take a breath before I speak.
To get a breath quickly, I breathe through the mouth.
I relax stomach muscles to give myself a deep enough breath.
I stop every time to take a breath before I read each of these lines.
I can use prose or poetry of any variety to practice breathing on my own.

Energetic Articulation

Tape-record yourself counting out loud from one to ten, using your normal articulation. Now mouth the numbers, using no breath or voice, exaggerating your articulation as if someone were lip-reading you from forty feet away. Keep this articulation relaxed as well as exaggerated, without stretching the mouth tensely. Be sure you release and drop your jaw naturally and easily, especially on the numbers "one," "five," "eight," and "nine."

Now repeat this exaggerated articulation with voice and again record the result. You should hear improvements in voice quality and clearness of articulation; both should contain a sound of energy and commitment. Repeat the exercise again, this time watching yourself in the mirror; your face should look natural and committed as you speak.

Repeat this exercise with a poem or a short prose selection. People who already have good resonance are often surprised to find that this energy in articulation gives them an extra measure of authority.

Projection

This exercise teaches you how to project your voice and give it volume without straining your throat. Many speakers have had the experience of a trip to the mountains in which they've stood at an overlook and called out, trying to get an echo in return. Most people project their voices beautifully at such times; they are relaxed, they take a deep breath of mountain air, open their mouths, and stretch out the vowel sounds as they call, "Hello-o-o-o out there!" Perhaps because they expect no response but their own echo, they don't strain their throats.

The calls of street vendors have to be heard in very noisy environments without throat strain or voice damage because for these street-corner merchants, their voices are their only form of advertising. Losing one's voice means being out of business, so a vendor usually uses relaxed, easy calls.

In the call "strawberries, apples, tomatoes," there are three different "a" sounds. Notice these sounds and repeat them, releasing and relaxing the jaw as you use the same three words. For this exercise imagine you're a street vendor selling his wares.

1. Do the call on a comfortably high pitch.
2. Repeat the call again at your lowest comfortable pitch without straining your throat to go lower than is comfortable.
3. Repeat the low-pitched call, but say "tomatoes" in a speech rhythm while maintaining the forward focus you used in calling it out.
4. Now take all three words to a speech rhythm, again maintaining the forward direction you used in calling the words. Don't stop between the words; keep them rolling. You are using good, easy projection.
5. Take the words of any speech and rehearse them through these steps. Your best projection and volume come without straining your throat.

With energetic articulation and the projection developed in this exercise, you should have sufficient volume for any situation. If listeners press you to speak louder at this point, you should use amplification equipment or suggest that the equipment you're using be checked. Don't try to do the impossible with your voice, because you could do serious damage to the vocal folds.

Resonance and Projection

With your body relaxed and in alignment, take a deep breath. Now say "mmm," concentrating the sound on your lips and teeth. Touch your lips with your fingertips—you should be able to feel the vibrations.

Now deliberately but gently try to force the "mmm" back in your throat. You can hear and feel the difference—the sound may be a bit choked and you will feel the pressure in your throat.

Once again, focus the sound on your lips and teeth. Your throat is again relaxed and open, the way it should always feel. Now match the "mmm" sound, still focused on the lips and teeth, with a series of vowels, each pronounced long:

"MmmAmā." Just relax your jaw, open your mouth and allow the "a" sound out.

"MmmAmē." Your jaw cannot drop far on this one.

"MmmAmȳ." Here your jaw does drop, way down.

"MmmAmō." Round your lips and drop your jaw.

String all these together and feel the constant buzzing in the front of the face as you say "mmma, mmme, mmmy, mmmo."

Now repeat the string at a faster speed, making sure you still feel the buzzing, and conclude with this short sentence: "We are too." The forward placement of your voice and the vibrations should feel the same as it did for the vowel string.

To carry over this full, easy resonance into daily conversation, you can use the "mmmhm" sound that most of us use to murmur agreement without interrupting a speaker. Using only the "mmmhms" you would normally use in conversation, you can monitor to see that the sound is placed well forward on the final "m." Listen to the next sentence you say; it should sound as if it is in basically the same place.

Open Your Mouth and Get Rid of Nasality

The following paragraphs have no nasal (m, n, or ing) sounds in them. You should be able to say them with your nostrils blocked with no difference in sound than if your nostrils were open. If you find as you block your nostrils with your fingertips that the sentences are plugged up in your nose, you know that you are saying them nasally. If this is the case, work at dropping your jaw to get your mouth open more. The object is to produce a fully oral tone.

Use your voice well. The work will reward you. Why are there speakers all are ready to follow? Others that bore us, or leave us doubts about their credibility? It is how you say what you say that decides how others react.

If you hold your voice back, if you have a tight jaw, you will look closed. You will look stiff. Your voice will be hard to hear. The vowels will have a flat quality. The look will say that you hide the truth. You are afraid to let go, to share what you have to say with others.

If you relax your jaw, you will have a fuller voice. If you really drop your jaw as you speak, you allow yourself to share your voice. The vowels will have a rich quality. Your voice will carry better as you let your voice out.

Downward Inflections

Practice saying the alphabet with upward inflections on each letter as you record your voice. Then record yourself again as you say the alphabet with downward inflections. The downward inflections, of course, will sound much more definite. Practice saying words in a series using downward inflections on every word:

One ↘ Two ↘ Three ↘
Reason ↘ Will ↘ Emotion ↘
Gold ↘ Silver ↘ Lead ↘

Now say a series of phrases with downward inflections:

This city needs improvements in education. ↘
In traffic control. ↘
In financial planning. ↘

Mark a prose passage or a speech for pauses. Record yourself, using upward inflections at the end of each phrase. Now record the same selection with downward inflections at the end of each phrase. Listen to the difference in the sound of authority.

Even questions demanding a yes or no answer sound better with downward inflections:

Would you like to become a better speaker? ↗

If this sentence is said with an upward inflection, it sounds as if you need someone's approval to continue your speech.

Would you like to become a better speaker? ↘

With a downward inflection, the same sentence sounds as though your advice is valuable and you believe people would benefit from hearing it.

If Your Voice Sounds Monotonous, Add Life

Choose a poem or a short prose selection, and monitor yourself with a tape recorder as you read it:

1. With no movement at all.
2. With large, exaggerated movements. Get your torso as well as your arms and hands involved in the movements. The movement creates vocal energy as your voice follows the lead of your movements. As a result your delivery has both excellent vocal energy and variety in vocal expression that is natural and spontaneous. Imposing changes in the pitch, rate, and volume of your voice without involving your body can sound studied and phony, but when the variety originates in movement, it always sounds real, because you are putting more of yourself into it.

As you apply this exercise to real speaking situations in your business life, you naturally should use movements appropriate to the situation. Larger-than-life sweeping movements may be fine for musical comedy or opera; much smaller ones are better for business.

Next, tape-record steps 1 and 2 of this exercise:

1. Say the word "no" as strongly as you can without movement.
2. Practice a karate chop or any aggressive, slashing motion of the arm and hand. Try to put your back into the movement.
3. Now say the word "no" as you use the motion you just practiced. Your "no" should have become much more energetic and forceful.

To develop an effective voice for speaking, you don't have to put in the hours at voice exercises that a singer or actor requires. But a little bit of practice with a tape recorder will go a long way toward making things happen with your voice. The exercises are meant to be just that—light workouts in the areas of your voice that need improvement. Just reading the chapter and skimming over the exercises won't open the door to changes in your voice; you have to hear the sound of your voice if you want to improve it. If you really want to make your audiences sit up and listen, a few extra minutes of work on this vital part of your spoken image can improve your effectiveness in every speaking situation.

CHAPTER TEN

Resistance

You now know all the techniques necessary to become a comfortable and effective speaker. This entire book is an effort to convince you that improvements in your planning and delivery are both possible and desirable. Yet most of us resist change, even when it means improvement, and our resistance can be a barrier to adopting new speaking habits. Trying something new demands that we test unfamiliar methods that can feel uncomfortable at first. We are reluctant to adopt a new style because we don't know for sure that it will work. We are anxious about adjusting a style that has brought us success, even if the adjustments would make us better. We sometimes resist getting in touch with ourselves, slowing down, and relaxing, because we see ourselves as hard-driving and intense. We all see ourselves in certain ways; change means altering that familiar picture and admitting to ourselves, perhaps, that we are not all that we could be.

We face resistance from outside as well. Listeners in a speaking situation also resist and have a right to do so, because the speaker makes demands on them, asking them to change in some way. An audience's resistance to the speaker is the normal resistance to unfamiliar or competing points of view.

Audiences resist in different ways—sometimes with anger and bitterness, but more often with a stubborn reluctance to be moved. This is passive resistance. It slows you down and, like quicksand, makes it harder to get where you want to go. Most business people experience some kind of passive resistance in almost every presentation they make, not because business people are disagreeable but because most business decisions must justify large investments of time, money, and manpower. Because of this, the average business speaker needs to focus on passive resistance rather than on confrontational styles of resistance that a political speaker would be more likely to encounter.

There will always be some degree of resistance in a speaking situation, and you ought to expect it, but it's more important that you deal with audience resistance in some situations than in others. The degree to which it matters depends on your Point X. A bank official speaking to civic club members about how to borrow money in a tight market may find that a fourth of his listeners disagree with his conclusions. Resistance from this audience, however, doesn't block his X, which is to present a point of view but not necessarily persuade the audience to accept that point of view. If the same bank official were speaking to the loan committee of his bank defending a loan he had made, he would be more concerned that the audience accept his views. Thus, if a fourth of this audience resisted, their resistance could interfere with his reaching his X and he would have to spend more time dealing with the resistance.

I was giving a videotape presentation to an audience of about two hundred potential clients when I was confronted with resistance from one member of the audience. The presentation was designed to show improvements that students had made in their speaking styles during a short time at Speakeasy. Before I could begin, however, I saw a hand waving wildly from the back of the room. A man leaped to his feet and asked in a belligerent voice,

"Under what conditions were these tapes made?" The tone of his voice said, "I don't believe what you're about to show me." I ignored the challenge and simply told him the tapes were made in Speakeasy's classrooms under normal conditions. Then I went ahead and showed them.

At the conclusion of the tape presentation, I was talking about the importance of body to spoken image when the same fellow jumped to his feet again. He said, "You don't mean to tell me that this body-image stuff is important, when everyone knows it's only mind control that counts." He was insisting on challenging me in front of two hundred people, and my first reaction was to cut him down. His own body image, after all, was tight and hyper, a good illustration of what I was talking about. But to cut him down, I would have had to make a fool of him in front of his colleagues, and I would have lost my authority by responding in that way. So I just looked at him and said, "A lot of people feel that mind control is important," and moved on. I didn't agree or disagree with him; I only recognized him with my comment and continued with my remarks.

If I had needed every person in the audience to agree with every word I was saying, I might have taken him on. But most of the people in the room seemed to agree with me, so resistance from one person didn't interfere with my objective. If the hand waver had been a student in a seminar, or one person in a group of five who really was having trouble understanding the importance of the body to speaking, then his resistance might have interfered with my ability to reach my X. I would have tried to learn why mind control was so important to him and why he was resisting the idea that body image was important.

Most business presentations are designed to persuade as well as inform. If your most frequent presentations are to clients or to in-house audiences, you will probably always be trying to move them in some way. So knowing how to deal with resistance is necessary if you are to become a better and more effective speaker.

Reducing Resistance in Your Content Planning

Your first opportunity to deal with resistance occurs during the planning stage, as you look at your content. Here, your most effective tool for reducing audience resistance is a thorough examination of your assumptions. If you organize your content according to the process in Part I, you should significantly reduce the potential for resistance from your listeners. Your Opening and your Message, especially, will be designed in terms of their needs and their situation. You increase audience resistance when your Point X asks or presumes too much, when you plan to move your audience too far.

Your Hidden X's—the personal and the business ones—can also increase audience resistance. Hidden X's can confuse, distract, or overwhelm your listeners. Since your Hidden X's consider only your own needs, you can easily overload your audience with too much content or divert them from your Point X with content that is irrelevant. In either case, a Hidden X that interferes with the ability of the audience to grasp your Message is a source of resistance. To decrease audience resistance in your content planning, you must have your Hidden X's under control.

Allen, the assistant director of a professional association, had just been appointed to succeed the retiring director. His predecessor was an excellent communicator, and Allen was attending courses so that he could do as well. He was also working on a master's degree at night and on weekends. To say he had a lot of irons in the fire is an understatement. His achievements and the frantic pace of his activities were all he talked about when he introduced himself to the group in the seminar.

Allen's style lacked energy, so I assigned him an energetic character to role-play. His choices were a carnival barker, a baseball manager disputing an umpire's call, or a panhandler. But when Allen came in on the day of the assignment, he proudly announced to the class, "I decided that instead of just doing one of the assignments, I would do all three."

It was obvious that Allen's personal Hidden X was to focus attention on his abilities. He needed his audience to know how much he could achieve. In doing the three assignments, he was saying in effect, "Look what I can do!"

In Allen's real speaking situations, the equivalent of doing three role plays would have been to overload his audience with content so they would know how smart he was. This Hidden X—to impress the audience with his intelligence and achievements—would create impatience and then resistance in any group.

Reducing Resistance with Your Style

Your speaking style can also raise or lower the audience's level of resistance. The lessons contained throughout Part II of this book on putting authority, energy, and audience awareness into your spoken image all are ways of reducing the likelihood of audience resistance.

Authority in your spoken image reduces resistance because it does not challenge or bully. It doesn't provoke your audience to fight back. Authority also means that you don't try to placate or cozy up to your audience; this would invite resistance by implying that the audience must like you in order to accept your Message.

Your energy makes it hard for an audience to resist getting involved with your presentation, for the simple reason that you are obviously involved in it. The energy shows the audience that you're committed to what you're saying and that it's worth their commitment, too.

Audience awareness decreases the chance or degree of resistance, because by being aware of the audience you communicate that you care about them. It's difficult to resist someone who demonstrates that he cares about you. Physically reaching out, with evident movement toward the people you are speaking to, is another way of showing them you care and inviting them to reciprocate. And audience awareness and its extension in active listening, a concept discussed fully later in this chapter, let you monitor resistance and deal with it before it becomes insurmountable.

Your Hidden X's can affect your style as well as your content and can raise or lower the amount of resistance you might expect from an audience. Allen, whose Hidden X directed a choice of content that increased resistance, also had a style that encouraged resistance. Although he spoke from a balanced body and had a smooth, articulate facade that conveyed authority and revealed no signs of nervousness, Allen didn't give out to his audience. He was just there. He gave no sign that he wanted to connect with the people who were listening. I pushed Allen to put energy into his voice and body. That's what he did in his three role plays, following instructions by putting a great deal of energy into each of the characters. His energetic performances showed his ability to master an assignment—but no commitment of his own energy to his audience or to an idea he believed in and wanted to share. His energy was self-focused, and his emphasis on himself continued to say, "Look what I can do!" when he should have been saying, "Look what we can share!" Allen's style would create resistance in the audience as soon as they realized that all his attention was directed to himself.

Techniques for Meeting Audience Resistance

It is not reasonable to expect that you will be able to breeze through all your presentations with no resistance whatsoever. The audience has the right to resist you as a speaker, because each party brings different needs to the speaking situation, and this means there will always be some level of resistance. But what happens when you've done everything possible in your content planning and your style to lower audience resistance and it meets you head-on anyway? Perhaps there's more resistance than you expected or it's different from what you expected. Maybe the resistance you're getting isn't even fair. You still have some choices in how you respond.

Changing Your Point X

Your first option is to change your Point X, making it less ambitious to account for the greater-than-expected resistance. This was something I should have done in a workshop on better speaking I once gave for midlevel hospital administrators. They listened politely all day long but asked very few questions. I had to work very hard to keep it going. As I thought about it later, I realized I had made a wrong assumption about them. I had assumed they wanted to be better speakers, but actually they were unaware of the importance of good communication to their success. As soon as I sensed their lack of commitment I should have scaled back my Point X. The result would have been less resistance from them and a more productive workshop.

An executive officer who tried to convince his board to buy an unprofitable company might also have fared better if he had scaled back his X to account for their resistance. Rather than going for broke and trying to win the conservative board's approval in one meeting, he would have been more realistic if he had limited his X to making them aware of the potential benefits of his proposal. He might then have reached his original X at a second meeting.

Many businesspeople may feel they have no choice about their Point X and couldn't change it or scale it down even if they wanted to. In that case, there are other options to explore when you face a lot of resistance.

Active Listening

Active listening is one of the most effective things you can do to overcome resistance. It is vital to a truly committed speaking style. Active listening means momentarily suspending your needs as a speaker to focus on the concerns of the audience. Carl Rogers, the man who first defined active listening, described it as listening without making judgments. He called it the greatest gift you can give someone. The actual techniques aren't as important as imagining what it would be like to be in the other person's shoes. You begin this by relaxing, pausing, and using eye contact to really see the audience, giving them the gift of your time to gain a better understanding of them.

I spoke about two years ago to a small group of sales managers. My topic was effective content organization for their business presentations, but when we met, they were distracted: it was between Thanksgiving and Christmas, the busiest time of year for these men and women: they were worried about slow Christmas sales, high inventories, and the fact that their company had told them to take time off to attend the workshop where I was one of several speakers. I knew in advance they'd be busy but thought they were ready to listen to what I had to say.

The sales managers resisted. They kept up a steady stream of questions, and insisted that I deal with specific cases from their business and then threw up reasons why what I was saying wouldn't work. It was very difficult to maintain a focus on what I wanted to accomplish with them. I couldn't abandon the Point X that had brought me there in the first place. But active listening told me why these hassled sales managers were distracted and gave me a choice about what to do next.

I decided to get right to the point. I said, "I want you to know that I realize you are very pressured right now and that business is hard. But I also have to say that I am not here as a business consultant to discuss your specific business needs. I'm here to tell you ways to organize your presentations that will make them easier and more effective. So let's move on, understanding that our purpose is to explore principles of presentation planning, not to deal with your specific business strategy." Being straight with the sales managers allowed me to stick to my original X.

Laying Your Cards on the Table

Laying your cards on the table, as I did with the sales managers, is an option that not every speaker is willing to take. But the more confidence you develop in yourself as a speaker, the more you may find it an attractive choice in dealing with resistance. Jake, a young lawyer, was speaking to executives of an electric utility in the weeks before a state legislature was to convene. His job was to give the utility executives tips for effective lobbying so they would be equipped to work against any antiutility legislation introduced in the pending session. Jake had had some political experience and was just beginning a promising career in law, and he wanted to be taken seriously. But the utility people made it clear from the beginning that because Jake didn't know a lot about their industry, they felt there was little he could tell them about lobbying on its behalf. Jake fought for their acceptance, but the harder he fought, the more they resisted and even baited him, and he found it impossible to get beyond the wall of their resistance.

Jake told me about his encounter with the utility executives several years later, when he was taking the seminar. "If I were doing it today," he said, "I think the audience would be the same—serious and inclined to resist what I was telling them. But I would certainly do some things differently. I wouldn't fight them, and I would level with them more. I believe I'd just tell them, 'I'm not an expert in your industry. I deal with many different industries and interest groups which need advice on lobbying. Here are the basic rules for lobbying effectively. If you want to try them, that's up to you, and if you don't, that's fine with me, too.'"

Jake, having developed confidence as a speaker and a professional, would have laid his cards on the table and stuck with his original Point X.

If scaling down or changing your X isn't possible or doesn't work, and the audience still resists; if active listening fails to provide the answer; if after you lay your cards on the table the audience continues to resist, you may decide you have but one option left.

Terminating the Speaking Situation

If you've thought about what matters to you and what you need from your listeners, you may decide that if the listeners don't want your content, then it's their problem, not yours. Sometimes, when you can't make contact no matter how hard you try, you have to make the decision that it's time to walk away.

Effective speakers always have to work and bend in order to reach their X. But you sometimes reach the point where you can bend and reach out no more—when you feel you are compromising your integrity and giving up who and what you are. You must then make a decision. If you are pursuing a client that you want at all costs, you may have to swallow his resistance. I believe, however, that when only one party tries to compromise, the relationship will never be successful. A business relationship won't work if you lose respect for yourself and the other person loses respect for you.

People deal differently with resistance, of course, because of their backgrounds—some people were raised in families and got into jobs where they've made a habit of saying yes all the time; they constantly swallow their pride and personality in order to get by. If this is what you have to do to make a situation work, you may have to ask yourself if it's worth it. If you have adapted and bent and the other person just won't move, there comes a point beyond which you give up who and what you are. Before you do that, you ought to walk away.

Now you've seen the choices you have for dealing with resistance you encounter in spite of your careful planning and effective style.

Be prepared to scale down or change your Point X.
Use active listening to detect underlying reasons for resistance.
Consider laying your cards on the table.
Be aware of your option to terminate the speaking situation.

Each of these choices is available. But your ability to choose the best response to resistance at the moment it happens depends on having your Hidden X's well under control.

Managing Resistance from Your Hidden X's

Most of the reasons for resistance come from inside of us. If we can deal with our Hidden X's, our presentations will probably be as effective and successful as they can be. The final responsibility for effectiveness lies within ourselves, not within the audience.

Most people look for resistance from the audience before they look for it in themselves. They want to know "What technique do you use when someone in the audience disagrees with you?" or, like one student who spoke in a tight voice with his shoulders squared and ready for action, "How do you handle those people in every audience who are out to get you?" What these speakers want is a list of techniques that will guarantee success any time there is any kind of resistance coming from any other person. They see resistance as a battle to be won or lost.

When a member of the audience resists, you cannot control or manipulate that person to bend her completely to your will. There are no formulas for dealing with various kinds of resisters. All you can change is you. The only choices you can control have to do with you. But by controlling yourself in the face of resistance, you can almost always control the situation and come away the winner.

People always seem to think there are rules for avoiding confrontation that will work no matter what. I've worked with a lot of people who know what they should do to keep from getting into confrontations with the audience, but the rules always seem to go out the window when they tighten up and lose control of their Hidden X's. None of the formulas ever worked for me, either, until I was ready to look to myself to see what I was fighting for, what mattered to me, or what I was afraid of losing. Unexpected or excessive resistance always puts pressure on your unstated needs from the situation, and your first response is likely to come from those needs. Unless you have them under control, you're not likely to choose the most effective way of dealing with the audience's resistance.

In my talk to the sales managers who were distracted by the Christmas business rush, for example, active listening let me understand the reasons they were distracted. So even though their comments and questions were aimed at me, I didn't take them as personally threatening or insulting. With my Hidden X's under control, I was able to make the right choice of responses— to encourage their attention by laying my cards on the table.

Jake, on the other hand, made the wrong choice in his encounter with the utility executives he was speaking to about lobbying. Their resistance threatened him and made it hard for him to control his personal Hidden X's, which at that point in his career were to have his advice accepted and to be respected as a professional. So he fought back, which caused his audience to escalate their resistance. You almost always increase resistance by viewing the speaking situation as a case of win-lose or as a battle, because it's in such cases that you're most likely to lose control of your Hidden X's.

You Don't Have to Fight to Win

I was recently in California for an appointment with the representative of a company interested in using me as a consultant. The final step in the approval process was meeting the vice-president in charge of marketing, and I reached his office about four-thirty on a Friday afternoon. He was sitting at his desk. He didn't rise to greet me but instead occupied himself shuffling papers and opening and closing the drawers in his desk. He acted very hassled and distracted, and informed me in a rushed, irritated voice, "We don't have very much time. I have to leave for a basketball game." The message I got from him told me that he considered himself far too important to be wasting his time with me on a Friday afternoon.

I felt my gut tighten, and my immediate reaction was to fight back. But I caught myself and thought, "Hold on. This is a no-win situation. If you try to beat this guy at his own game, you can't be yourself and you'll lose." I exhaled to relax and repeatedly told myself to slow down and stay calm as I kept looking at him. As I looked at him, I talked slowly and rationally at the side of his head while he fished around in his desk drawers and asked questions in his hurried, harried voice. As I continued to talk and look at him, however, he began to slow down and listen. Soon he stopped rummaging among his papers and became attuned to me, and we had a satisfactory conversation.

This was an interesting lesson to me, because by not fighting the battle, I had won the war—I had reached my Point X. By remaining slow, steady, direct, and calm, and maintaining my focus, I made it very difficult for him to resist being pulled in. By reaching out, I managed to bring my audience of one into my atmosphere.

When I walked into his office, active listening let me see that he was insecure and had a need to let me know that he was in control and could push me around. I gained insights that helped me know how to react in order to control the situation. My choice of reactions turned out to be the right choice under the circumstances. But if my original choice to be calm and reasoned and to bring him into my atmosphere had failed, I could still have made the choice to walk out. When Carl Rogers said that active listening is the greatest gift you can give someone, he might have added that it's also a great gift to give yourself in a speaking situation.

Active listening gives you information that can help you win without fighting. The other person's major need may be to feel in control, even if it's temporary and illusory; if you deny him that by fighting back he'll fight even harder. Soon a simple situation that can be dealt with easily and painlessly escalates into a confrontation, and nobody wins. If you can simply listen, avoiding the critical self-judgment that you're giving up control and letting someone push you around, what you're really doing is controlling yourself. By holding on to who and what you are, you can usually prevail. This means also avoiding the value judgment that the person resisting is a fool or a boor who needs to be put down just to satisfy your ego; if indeed she is, she will almost certainly reveal it without your help.

Listen to Yourself

The episode with the hand waver also showed me the value of pausing to look inward, of trying to understand my reactions to certain situations. In making the choice to avoid a fruitless battle,

I gained an important source of information from pausing to listen to myself. The presentation was on the West Coast, two thousand miles and three time zones away from my home. I had arrived late the night before. The airline had lost my luggage, including papers I needed for my presentation. I was physically exhausted and mad at the world when I woke up the next day. Because I realized this, I took a quiet walk and did some breathing. I tried to listen to myself, and what I heard was, "Sandy, you'd better be careful today. You're tired, you're on edge, you're mad at the airline and the world in general. If anybody looks at you wrong today, you're going to want to fight." In other words, my Hidden X was to take out my frustrations on the first person who crossed me. So when I saw that aggressive wave from the back of the room, I was able to remind myself, "Watch it. Take it slow. Think of what you're going to say before you say it."

Taking the time to listen to yourself is just as important as listening to your audience, so that you understand your reactions under stress and remember that on certain days you are more likely to get caught up in battle. When you listen to yourself and react to the information you receive, you are recognizing and controlling your Hidden X's.

Because people don't agree with us one hundred percent doesn't mean they oppose us completely. Speaking is not a battle with the audience to be won or lost. You don't have to take a step toward confrontation when you deal with resistance from the audience. Confrontation supposes that your differences are greater than your common ground. Fighting with the audience enlarges the differences, letting them grow bigger and bigger until there's no way you can get beyond them to your Point X. Avoiding the conflict keeps you on course toward your X, and you can do this only when you are in control of your Hidden X's.

You now know a variety of ways in which to deal with resistance—you can ignore it if it doesn't interfere with reaching your

X; adjust your X; ask questions of the audience; focus on audience needs with active listening; or lay the cards on the table. Finally, you can decide that you have to walk away.

But just as there are no pat formulas for the right way to speak, there is no formula for dealing with resistance. We each bring our strengths and weaknesses, our own tension levels, our own styles of listening, to the speaking situation. The more you understand yourself and what you need from your audience—your own Hidden X's—the better you are able to handle resistance.

You should understand that there will always be some resistance. It is the audience's right to resist, and you should expect resistance. You can only really control and change yourself. But with the right kind of planning and the right kind of delivery you can greatly reduce the likelihood that your audience's resistance will prevent you from getting the results you want.

Part III

SPECIAL COMMUNICATION SITUATIONS

CHAPTER ELEVEN

Large Meetings

Meetings are a fact of life for all of us. Much of a businessperson's week is taken up by small group meetings of one sort or another—informational meetings, brainstorming meetings, decision meetings. And, in spite of the fact that most of the major decisions that impact a company's success are made in small group meetings, it's usually the large meetings that get the attention—events like customer appreciation meetings, partnership meetings, quarterly sales meetings. They typically have multiple speakers and hundreds, even thousands, of people in the audience. Often lasting for days, these meetings cost a lot of money, both in terms of the expenses of the meeting itself and in terms of the time spent in planning and attending them.

Considering the investment they represent, it's surprising how ineffective so many large meetings are. Or maybe not so surprising. After all, the obstacles to a successful large meeting are formidable: a lot of people involved, both planning the meeting and speaking at it, each with his or her own agenda and focus; a lot of technology and "bells and whistles," which offer a significant challenge to coordinate and which often intimidate or overwhelm the individual speaker. And, although the changing business environment is forcing more people to be open to new ways of doing things, there are still some habits about large meetings that persist—expectations about what topics are covered, who should speak, and how each day is organized.

So I suppose the real surprise, given all these obstacles, is that any large meeting is effective. Yet some are, providing rewarding experiences for those attending and moving the companies themselves closer to their goals. What makes the difference? In my work with clients I've found that much of what you've already read in this book, about planning and delivering an effective individual presentation, can be applied to large meetings as well. Sure, there have to be adjustments and modifications. Even compromises. But the basic principles remain the same. And they can make a huge difference.

Planning the Large Meeting

Point X—Plus . . .

Just as in the planning for an individual presentation, the planning for a large meeting starts with a definition of your Point X, only now for the entire meeting: "At the end of this meeting, my listeners will. . . ." For example, "At the end of this meeting the attendees will be prepared to implement their part in our new technology initiative." Or, "At the end of this meeting the attendees will demonstrate their commitment to our business partnership by volunteering to serve on practice area advisory committees."

But there are two very important, additional characteristics of this Point X for a large meeting. The first is that it must be set with a view to the larger context. There's really no reason to have a large meeting today unless it's tied into the business goals of the organization. People spend a lot of energy, time, and money on large meetings without thinking about results in the way they do when they go into a five-person meeting to persuade their listeners to buy something or approve something. Large meetings should have an X that aligns with the business strategy—the company's movement forward. So when you plan a large meeting, you need to ask yourself what you can make happen through communication that will cause the listeners to move closer to your business goals. And I believe it is possible for even huge audiences to move through a thought and belief process in the course of a well-planned meeting.

That's one thing your overall Point X for the meeting must take into account. It's part of a larger context. It is, in effect, an interim X along the path toward your company's business goals. The second important additional characteristic of the large meeting X is ownership. There is often a planning committee for large meetings. But no matter how big or small this group is, someone has to accept ultimate responsibility for the meeting's success. Ideally, this should be a senior-level person who is a firm believer in results-oriented communication.

The role of the meeting owner is to "endorse and enforce." First of all, the owner decides on or signs off on the overall Point X for the meeting. Second, he or she has the authority and the willingness to keep all the elements of the meeting on track toward that X.

I've certainly seen what can happen when there is no ownership for a meeting. You get planning by committee. Those assigned the task of planning the meeting sit around and everyone volunteers what he or she thinks the X should be. Often, even unconsciously, they lose sight of the bigger picture and the larger context and are driven by their own agendas. The result is an X that tries to make everybody happy. It's not focused, and consequently the potential power of the meeting is never realized.

This problem can be avoided when one person, who understands the meeting's function, takes ownership.

Don't get me wrong here. I'm not suggesting that the owner for the meeting is a kind of dictator, imposing his or her view on everyone else. A good planning process will include a lively discussion and debate about the purpose of the meeting and of what's most important to accomplish through it. But at some point a decision must be made—and agreement, once reached, must be enforced. That's the role of the meeting owner, and of his or her designated representatives.

Once the overall X for the meeting has been set, all the other decisions about the meeting, whether made by a committee or a coordinator, are driven by it: Who should be speaking. What they should be speaking about. The format of the meeting. A woman involved in the planning of large meetings for an international consulting company describes the effect of defining an overall X this way:

> Once we set the X, we had some very intense discussions about what things should be covered. We put things into the meeting we might not otherwise have included, because getting to X required it. The X also gave us a basis for questioning those routine standing topics. When someone said, "Well, we usually open the meeting with a report on such and such," you have to ask, "How does that advance us toward our X?"

Each Speaker's Part—Two Models

Once you have defined your overall X for the meeting, one aligned with your business goals and owned by someone at the highest level, you're ready to consider the content of each speaker's part in the meeting. There are two ways of doing this—a simple way and a more complex way.

Let's start simple. You can design a presentation according to the planning process outlined in Part I of this book. You have your X for the meeting. Develop a Message that targets on that X, a Message for the whole meeting. (Sometimes this will be expressed as a "theme.") Then determine what questions are raised by that Message. Each speaker's assignment is to answer one of those questions. You'll remember that, within the individual presentation, the answer to each question is itself a "minimessage"; so, for a large meeting with multiple speakers, each of those minimessages becomes a main Message for each individual speaker. It's as simple as that.

This simple model will only work when one person or a small group has significant influence over every piece of the meeting. Recently, the head of sales for a division of a multinational company asked for my help with his large sales meeting. He sent me an agenda, which was basically a list of topics. It was a very busy time for me, so I phoned him and spent fifteen minutes explaining the concept of Point X to him, and then sent him the chapters on presentation planning from this book.

I have to admit I was really surprised at his commitment. Within days I got back from him a description of an X for the meeting, a Message for the meeting, and a list of questions raised by the Message. Because it was clearly his meeting, and the subject area was rather narrowly focused, it was possible for us to use the simple model and assign the speakers to answer those questions. In fact, specific speakers were chosen based on their ability to address a particular question and answer. These were not in every case the same speakers he had originally chosen when his agenda for the meeting was just a list of topics.

But most large meetings are more complicated—starting with the fact that several people may have decision-making responsibility for them. They involve multiple speakers, including outside speakers, some of whom have to be booked months before the hard planning for the meeting begins—in other words, before the overall X is determined. These meetings usually include videos and some "entertainment" elements. They often have small breakout sessions. So the simple model for assigning roles and content for the meeting just won't work.

But you can still use the process. Each element of the meeting—the speakers, the videos, the breakout sessions, even the "fun" activities—needs to have its own X, one that is designed and understood as an interim X moving the participants ever closer to the overall meeting X.

Let's take an example. You've decided that your overall X for the meeting is that the people "will be prepared to implement their part in our new technology initiative." Now you've decided that, to reach that goal, there are at least three critical steps the people must take. The first is understanding what the technology initiative is. The second is believing that the initiative is important to the company's (and their) future. The third step is understanding and then accepting their role in the process—in how they get there. There are two key parts to this step. The first is people; that is, what kind of people will be needed to ensure the initiative's success? The other part is organization: How do we need to be organized in order to implement this initiative?

Each of these steps would represent a part of the meeting and each would have its own X. Suppose you've already contracted with an outside speaker who's an expert in market research, and she's scheduled for the second day, which you've assigned to the "people" issue. Since you've already identified the importance of hiring and retaining a certain type of person for your initiative, you would ask her to focus her talk on what her research has discovered about the characteristics of these people: what they value and what kind of communication they tend to respond to. In this way you've made sure that your outside expert contributes to the interim (people) X and to the overall X for the meeting.

You also want each person to think about how his or her current work process and structure might have to be modified to better support this new initiative. So you schedule a breakout session during the "organization" part of the meeting, and have as your X for the session that the participants will leave it having identified one of two changes they need to make in the way they're organized. With this X you have a clear target to help you design the session.

Perhaps in the segment on the importance of the initiative, you've given your creative people the assignment to produce a video with the X so that, at the end of it, the viewers will feel excited about the possibilities this new initiative will open up for the company. With this as their focus, the production experts can unleash their imaginations to create a vision of the future. It could be fun, or challenging, or inspiring—it can be anything as long as it targets on that X.

I hope this gives you some sense of how even the most diverse elements of a large meeting can still work together to achieve a very clearly defined goal. But I don't want to make it sound easy. For some years I have been advising the head of a company on his annual meeting, which is a three-day affair attended by over four thousand people. Initially, I struggled with some of the problems I've already mentioned here: no owner for the meeting, every person seeing a different part of the pie, each element of the meeting being an isolated piece of communication. A couple of years ago we began to change that. We put one senior executive in charge of the meeting and then formed a planning group. Part of the planning group was the "content committee," which I led.

The meeting was scheduled for June. By January our content committee had come up with an X that the senior person believed in and took ownership for. We had roughed up an agenda targeted on that X. We had identified the Messages and tentatively assigned the internal speakers. As part of their contract with us, the outside speakers had to agree to use our planning process. We understood, of course, that these outside speakers already had most of their own content, but we helped them shape it for our goals and our context. (We actually assigned a content committee member to each outside speaker.) We also communicated very clearly to the production companies and creative houses what their X's were, as well as the overall meeting X that they were supporting.

Now, I won't pretend that everyone signed on to the process right away. There was, initially, resistance to what some felt was too much control. But we reduced that through a combination of education and support. We explained the overall goal of the meeting and their individual contribution to reaching it. Then we provided each speaker with a "sample" of what his or her talk would look like, with its own X and Message. They had ample opportunity to interact, object, and modify; but, in fact, they actually appreciated the help and direction. They were very busy people who resisted control but appreciated support. They especially liked feeling part of a team working to accomplish a clearly articulated goal. Each year the planning of this meeting gets easier, as more people understand the process and experience the positive results of it for themselves and the company. Here's how one member of our committee described the results of the new planning process:

> For the first time we really put rigor into the three days of meeting, and the audience response was wonderful. In the post-event surveys people consistently commented on how much they liked the focus. They also recognized the work that went into the agenda. Most of all, everyone left that meeting with something to accomplish—with a sense of what their next step or steps were, for the business. And because our X's had taken account of the emotional component of the issues, they left motivated to take those next steps.

When you get results like that, it makes all the hassles worthwhile.

Benefits of the Planning Process

It isn't always easy to get the cooperation and commitment needed to plan a successful large meeting. And there will always be disappointments, like speakers who, despite your best coaching and clearest direction, still insist on doing their own thing. But the benefits of careful planning, both for the individuals who attend the meetings and the companies who mount them, are worth the effort. In my work with many companies over the years, I've witnessed very significant benefits. Here are some of them:

- *This planning process gets differences out in the open.* The more people involved in the meeting, the more different opinions you'll have about what the meeting is for, what you should try to accomplish, what the audience needs or wants. And there will always be those who can't imagine having a whole meeting on only "one thing." But the process of selecting a single X for the meeting moves the discussion to a higher, more strategic level. It forces people to choose, for themselves and for the organization, the most important result for this communication event. Priorities emerge and compete. Each interest has to make its case. In the end, the process is actually energizing for those involved. And the overall X that emerges is not a committee X, but a true consensus, with the kind of buy-in needed to drive all the other decisions about the meeting.

- *This planning process can be a great management tool leading up to the meeting.* Once the overall X is determined, and a tentative agenda with interim X's is developed, certain gaps will emerge. They could be anywhere—in the degree of awareness of the participants, in the information available to the speakers, or in the state of a particular project that getting to your X depends on. The meeting date then becomes a target, by which some very specific things need to be done. Perhaps a particular project must have been completed or have reached a certain stage; perhaps the attendees will need to have preliminary discussions of some issue in advance; perhaps some data needs to be captured or analyzed in a different way. If your overall meeting X has been aligned with your organization's goals, then filling in these gaps is not just contributing to the success of the meeting; it's contributing to the success of the business as well.

- *This planning process releases creativity.* Again and again I've witnessed how this process opens people up. Once you have your X, organizing the meeting to get there can often be fun. Anything is allowed as long as it contributes to the movement toward that X: an unusual speaker; a different format for breakout sessions; some unusual entertainment at the cocktail hour; or a new spin on the usual prizes or awards. The people with production houses really appreciate being given their X's. It provides them a focus for their work and stimulates their creativity. On more than one occasion I've seen them come back with ideas for additional elements that would contribute to reaching an overall X.

- *This planning process saves time.* There are no shortcuts to planning a large meeting, but there are efficiencies. When everyone is using the same language and the same planning process, it's quickly apparent where someone has gone off track or where there are gaps to be filled. And the most important aspect of this common language is that it's results-oriented. You're never asking someone what she is going to be talking about (her subject); rather, you're asking what is her X, how does that X prepare her listeners for the next element of the meeting, and how does it move her listeners closer to the overall meeting X.

I'll let one of the members of my content committee at the consulting firm sum up the benefits of using this planning process for large meetings. According to him, "When you get it right, the participants really engage. They feel good about the time spent in the meeting. And the sponsor of the meeting can see whether they got the results they wanted."

One final note: Although I've focused on the benefits of planning for large meetings in this chapter, it's just as important to use this planning process for small group meetings. This is where, as I've said, the most significant decisions are usually made.

Speaking at the Large Meeting

If you're like most businesspeople, your most common communication situations are in small group settings, or one-on-one. Your experience in front of a really large audience is relatively limited. So just the size of the audience at a large meeting can be a bit intimidating. Then, too, at a company or divisionwide meeting, there are probably people in the audience really important to you, people who can affect your career. Now add all the technology—speech prompters, video magnification, computer graphics. So much to take into account; so much to go wrong.

All of this means that you're likely to feel an increased level of stress if you're on the agenda for a large meeting. It's important to recognize this, to tune in to yourself. Consider with more care than usual your Hidden X's for this occasion, and take the time to reduce your stress by using the techniques I discussed in the chapter "Speaking Without Fear."

The qualities of an effective style—authority, energy, and audience awareness—are just as important for you at a large meeting as they are in front of a small group. But there are some features of a large meeting that put extra pressure on these qualities, and I've seen some speakers, who are usually very effective in smaller situations, lose much of that effectiveness when they stand up in front of a thousand people. It doesn't have to be that way.

The Challenge to Authority

Many companies put on real extravaganzas when they bring large groups of people together. They feature slick motivational videos, multiscreen graphic presentations, and even live orchestras. When the purpose is something as important as, for example, the announcement of a new marketing campaign, the meeting can take on the fully scripted and choreographed aspects of a Broadway show—complete with a producer and director. In this kind of situation, it's easy for you as an individual speaker to feel like a cog in the machinery; sometimes, indeed, the people in charge of the meeting treat you that way, scheduling your rehearsal whenever it fits their production schedule and interrupting you while you're rehearsing to adjust the lighting, the microphone, the TelePrompTer, or some other element of the "set."

Authority starts in your head. You can deliver your talk with authority only if you feel important. No matter how many speakers are on the agenda or how much production is involved, you as an individual speaker have your moment to make a difference. To move the meeting, and the audience, one step closer to the final Point X. So stay focused on the importance of your role to the meeting's success, and make sure that you rehearse *in the space* often and long enough to feel like you own it—to reach the point of feeling that all the technology and production elements are supporting you, not competing with you.

I remember watching an executive rehearse her speech, which was on a prompter, on the eve of a large meeting. She was working with the meeting producer, and she read her speech off the prompter straight through, without errors. The producer walked up to her afterward offering congratulations. "You were terrific," he told her. "That's it." But it was clear to me that she wasn't really settled and comfortable in the space. On the first run-through with the prompter she was letting it lead her through her talk. She wasn't in charge, and her voice and body were not yet saying, "I have a right to be here." So I told her, "You need more rehearsal." And she agreed.

The meeting producer was concerned with coordinating the graphics and the flow of the talk, and because the speaker managed to get through without stumbling and all the cues were in the right place, he was satisfied. But the speaker and I were looking for much more than a smooth flow. We were looking for a speaker with the kind of presence that would make the large number of people in the audience sit up and listen. That was just as important as the "production."

The Challenge to Energy

The "production" aspect of large meetings can also affect your energy as a speaker. You can become so focused on following the prompter or making sure your words are in sync with the graphics that your energy level drops. What energy you have is directed toward "things," not people. Don't let this happen.

It's important to remember that a large audience needs a lot of energy from you. There are so many distractions in a large meeting, not only on the stage but in the audience itself: production people moving about, attendees coming and going, whispering to each other, rustling notes or checking the agenda to see who or what's next. The people in the seats really need your energy to pay attention. So think "bigger"; work hard to project even more energy than you would use in a smaller group.

But energy, especially in a large meeting, isn't just about

projecting and filling up the room. It's not just about delivering your content with commitment. All this is important, but in a deeper sense, your energy is your expression of who you are, your "aliveness" in the room. It expresses your engagement with whatever is going on while you're speaking. A twinkle in the eye at something amusing; a flash of excitement when you make a crucial point or get a positive response from your listeners; even a rueful smile when you stumble over a phrase or the wrong visual comes up. Expressing energy means bringing your unique life into that room and allowing yourself to express it. This is especially important in large meetings where the speaker is video-magnified on a screen. However small you may feel on a big stage in front of a large audience, they see you bigger than life, and if you shut down or stiffen up, you'll come across as uncomfortable or, even worse, as inauthentic, someone playing a role.

The Challenge to Awareness

You're on the stage, at the lectern. Behind you, your own face is magnified on a large screen. Out in front of you are a set of speech prompters. Bright lights come down into your eyes. Somewhere out there, beyond all this stuff, is your audience, numbering maybe in the thousands.

It's no wonder that a lot of speakers in this situation decide that either it's not possible or not important to see their audience. Except for those in the front rows, most are a blur beyond the lights. And, anyway, there are so many of them you couldn't possibly see them all. As long as you look out generally in their direction, they won't know the difference, right?

Wrong. They'll know. They'll hear the difference in the tone of your voice, and they'll see it in the video magnification—the expression on your face that says, "I'm not really talking to anyone."

I won't deny that it's a lot harder to have audience awareness in a large meeting situation. And I'll agree that it's often not possible to see everyone in the audience. But the important thing to remember is that awareness is not just a physical act, it's an intention. Your voice and facial expressions become more lively and more real when you *try* to see a listener, when you *make the effort* to see or to visualize a real live person listening to your words.

Try to have the lights adjusted, both for brightness and location, so that it's easier to see your audience. Then, as you talk, really look out and try to focus on individuals. They will sense your intention and experience the difference in many subtle, but critical, ways in your delivery. And you'll get an added benefit called the "halo effect." When you attempt to focus on a single, albeit indistinct individual out in the audience, many of the people around him or her will feel like you're actually talking directly to them.

I'll never forget a large meeting when the speaker really used his audience awareness to wonderful effect. The occasion was the centennial anniversary celebration for a big international corporation. The audience was fourteen thousand people, plus five thousand more watching on video from another location. The final talk of this four-day meeting was given by the CEO. His awareness of his audience had started with the content. There were jokes about the hotels way outside the city that people had to stay at. There were references to episodes of lost luggage. He commented about the difficulty of finding your way around all this maze of people. He was really talking to them.

Way up in the front of the hall in a raised area behind the stage, there was a large group of people who could only see the speakers' backs; for most of the meeting they had been looking at monitors. During his talk the CEO actually turned around and walked back in their direction. He joked with them about being higher up there in the gallery than they had been in the airplane coming to the meeting. He suggested that they should have been provided magazines. It was all done with humor, but he was demonstrating his awareness of everyone in his audience—even those who couldn't see him! And he was saying, in effect, "I see you. I know you haven't had the best seats all week, but I still think you're terrific."

There was also an unplanned moment in his talk when he mentioned something about the headaches people must have had during the week. Suddenly, there was some tittering in the audience. In an audience of fourteen thousand, with all those cameras going and the lights in his eyes, the CEO heard the slight noise, stopped, looked in the direction of it, and asked, "I suppose some of you have a headache now, right?" Then there was a spontaneous explosion of laughter and agreement.

Now, that meeting was a very big event. Everyone who attended came away with many special memories. But even now, years later, people remember that speech as a highlight of the event. I believe it was because they felt really seen and acknowledged by that CEO.

In fact, his speech is a good example of all the basic qualities of an effective style. There were plenty of expensive audiovisuals and sophisticated multimedia presentations. But this man was using himself. He owned the space and moved all over it, even into the audience at one point. He used his energy to engage all those thousands of people, pretty tired by that point in the meeting. And his awareness made each person feel individually valuable. This was a speaker who walked into the room that afternoon believing he could have an impact. And he did.

You can, too, even in a large meeting.

CHAPTER TWELVE

Communicating Through Technology

Success in a large meeting depends on your ability to impose yourself and make the connection. But today that success often has to be achieved in a new and very different arena—one defined by the new communication technology.

For many years technology has been used to add glitz and energy to meetings. It's been in the service of the big production. The listeners were truly an "audience" for a performance that was planned months in advance. In that kind of environment (which still exists at many companies for certain large meetings), the speaker really has a "role" and has to work hard not to be subordinated to the production.

But the newer technology is quite different. It offers real-time communication across vast distances and multiple media for that communication (voice, video, written). It allows, even encourages, more immediacy and spontaneity in the communication. And listeners are expecting more participation—as they are doing in so many other aspects of their lives through technology. So you can forget scripting everything in advance and expecting that it will all go as planned. Of course it's important, and always will be, to rehearse and to feel as comfortable as possible with anything you're using in your communication; however, what ultimately determines your effectiveness in this new arena is how authentic you can be, how present and responsive to the listeners as you're speaking.

This is a remarkable and powerful shift in the uses of technology for communication, and it dramatically increases the demands on any speaker. It requires a very firm grasp of the X for the communication, because the greater immediacy and participation will always threaten a loss of focus or a change in direction. It demands a strong personal authority, because the interactive environment tends to put all participants on the same level. And successful speakers in this new environment will have to reach out for the connection more directly than ever, because audience members will expect to be seen and interacted with as individuals more than ever before.

Let me give you some specific examples of this new communication environment—taken from what I've seen my clients do during the past year.

- Videoconferencing. This technology is not particularly new, but more businesspeople are using it because it's easier and less expensive than it used to be, both in terms of the equipment needed and the cost of satellite time. And it's being used in more ways. I have "sat in" on meetings, coached a client for an upcoming presentation, and participated in a strategic planning session, all from a remote location.
- "Chat room" participation in a large meeting. One client conducted a meeting with a relatively small group on site but which was satellite-broadcast to a much larger number at about twenty remote locations. The interesting technological feature of this meeting was the number of channels of communication: in addition to the real-time broadcast and a telephone hookup, there was also a computer "chat

room." At each location some of the participants were at computer terminals inputting their reactions to and comments about the proceedings of the meeting. A person in a control booth at the primary site was assigned to monitor and read these comments; from time to time the broadcast would switch to him and he would share some of them.

- "Response system." One client was dealing with some issues that required both a quick decision and general support in the firm; they chose a technology for their meeting that would give all the participants the opportunity to share their feelings and opinions about the issues. The speakers presented each issue for about twenty-five minutes and then gave the audience a chance to select one of three options for dealing with it. Every participant at the meeting had buttons to press to indicate his or her preference. The results were instantly tabulated and appeared on a screen as bar graphs.

These examples illustrate the more immediate and interactive quality of communication technology today. This technology is a wonderful resource but, as I said, it also places more demands on any speaker who wants to use it effectively. One such demand, and a critical one, is establishing and maintaining a clear focus for the communication. That, as you know by now, is the purpose of your X.

Technology and Your X

As companies become more global, videoconferencing becomes a very cost-effective alternative to travel when you want to have a meeting. You can meet with people in Madrid, London, and New York all at the same time. Decisions can be made; next steps can be agreed upon. But I believe it's even more critical to have a clearly defined X for the meeting when it is videoconferenced.

First of all, it's important to have an X because, though video-conferencing is less expensive than it used to be, it's still not cheap, and no company can afford to waste money on an unpro-ductive videoconferenced meeting. So having a definite X will lead you to a series of key questions; for example: Is a meeting the best format to accomplish this X? And, who really needs to be at this meeting in order to accomplish this X?

Answering these questions should reduce the number of video-conferenced meetings and keep down the number of participants at each meeting. All businesspeople complain about the number and length of meetings they attend. They are too often unfo-cused, inefficiently run, and unproductive. One common problem with meetings is that too many people are invited to attend. Videoconferencing can aggravate this problem because it vastly expands the potential number of meeting participants. And, because not every person is in the same room, it increases the ten-dency of the mind to wander and the energy level of the partici-pants to drop.

It's hard to keep a discussion focused and energy flowing when everyone is not physically in the same room and when the num-ber of participants is large. In my experience videoconferencing works best when there is intense dialogue back and forth with only a few people at each location—and when the meeting is driven by one or two people who have a clear understanding of the X. The larger the group and the less clear the focus, the more difficult it is to achieve something.

So, in the case of videoconferencing, your decision to use it should be driven by the same kinds of considerations you would use for any meeting; the technology is merely a convenience for the participants and a potential cost-saving for the company. If you keep the number small and the focus firmly on your X, it can be a very useful communication resource. But there is one case for which I would not recommend it. If your X has a strong emotional component, try to have all the meeting participants together in the same room.

Two Experiences in the Chat Room

Remember my example of the meeting with the "chat room" component? There were actually two such meetings conducted by the same company, and the first of those meetings was a perfect illustration of a technology divorced from any clearly defined X for the occasion. The chat room became an alternative communication channel parallel to the broadcast program. I remember sitting at a table in one of the remote locations looking at the speaker on the screen. Suddenly, I heard this burst of laughter from someone farther down my table. It certainly wasn't at something the speaker was saying. Then I noticed he was reading his laptop screen. When I went and looked over his shoulder, I saw that the chat room was full of responses from the listeners—irreverent, funny, questioning. But, although the person monitoring the chat room comments at the broadcast site would occasionally share some of them, they were not really integrated into the program itself. It was as if the listeners were talking to each other behind the speakers' backs. My question was echoed by a comment from one of the chat room participants: "What the heck is the X of this broadcast?"

The second chat room meeting was quite different and much more successful. The meeting had been planned for some weeks and the CEO was very clear on his X for it: After the meeting the participants all over the world would have a deepened commitment to the new company strategies. Facilitators were assigned at each of the remote locations to continue the discussion after the

broadcast and to develop specific action steps with the participants at that site.

But just a few days before the scheduled broadcast, the CEO
announced a significant organizational change. He knew that
there would be considerable interest in and even some concern
about the change, and so he incorporated some comments about
it at the top of the meeting and announced that thirty minutes
would be dedicated at the end of the meeting to deal with any
questions.

The broadcast then proceeded as planned, while the tele-
phoned questions were being recorded and the chat room
responses and concerns monitored. What soon became clear was
that all the questions were about the organizational change,
none about the strategies. At one point, while a video was playing, the studio director huddled with the CEO to inform him of
what was coming in from the sites. At that point the CEO made
a courageous decision. He adjusted his X to take account of the
listeners' reality, because he understood that there was no way
they would commit to the strategies until their concerns about
the organization were dealt with. When the live broadcast
resumed—about fifty minutes into a two-hour meeting—he
announced that the rest of the time would be devoted to answering their questions.

Now this CEO didn't completely abandon his original X: First
of all, he knew that the facilitators were in place to focus on the
strategies after the broadcast; second, whenever it was appropriate, he referred to the strategies during the Q&A. For example, in
response to a question about whom he might appoint to a particular position in the new organization, he declined to give a specific
name (saying he wasn't yet ready to do that), but made the point
that whoever was appointed would be someone who understood
the new strategies and was really committed to them. In this way

he kept his ultimate X clear in his own mind and in front of his listeners.

What was different in this second chat room meeting was that the conversation in the chat room was integrated into the meeting process. Even more, it significantly altered that process. In order for this to be negotiated successfully, the CEO needed more than the courage to shift gears and deal with current reality. He also needed a firm grasp of how an X functions in a communication situation. It was this grasp that made him understand that, in order to accomplish his ultimate X for the meeting, he needed to focus on an interim X. The participants had to be more comfortable with the organizational change before they would commit more deeply to the new strategies. In other words, he revised the meeting in the service of his X. And the technology both helped alert him to the need to revise, and provided the means to do it effectively.

How Much Interaction Do You Want?

What I think is especially interesting about these chat room examples is that they illustrate the interactive quality of so much of the new communication technology. It creates greater possibility for audience or listener participation and response, and often in an immediate way. Listeners were never really passive; but the new technology is making listeners more active. This is, on the whole, a positive development, but it makes the issues of control and focus more urgent. Hence the importance of a clear X. Then you can decide how much "interactivity" you need and where you will need it.

Let's say, for example, that you're having a meeting with your sales force and the subject is a new commission structure. You want to be sure they all understand it. Your X is, "As a result of this meeting, there will be no questions from the field about how we arrived at the figures on their checks at the end of this month." You may decide that an interactive component, by video or audio or computer, will enhance your prospects for accomplishing that X. You could present some sample situations and ask the listeners to figure out the commission and then respond. You could give credit by name to the first one with the right answer. You might invite the sales force to give you problems or to ask you questions. The point is that the technology should be in the service of your X. If the new commission structure is unpopular but nonnegotiable, it would be important to control the interactive environment so that it did not become a gripe session.

The "response system" meeting I witnessed—where the participants voted their preferences on some issues—was an effective use of interactive technology in the service of a clearly defined X. The CEO had just been appointed a few days before, and it was important that decisions be reached that had maximum support within the company. The vote with the instant graphic representation was a perfect way to accomplish this goal. The process of participation helped ensure that even those who disagreed with the outcome of any particular vote would be more likely to accept it.

Now this form of interactive technology wouldn't be a good choice if, for example, the issues were too divisive or too complex to be reduced to a simple choice between two or three options. Or when you're not committed to accepting the results of a vote that everyone sees. I can imagine a situation where the choice of this interactive technology could be driven by a Hidden X, and where it would end up sabotaging the accomplishment of your real X. Suppose your real X was that after the meeting the participants would support three key decisions the executive committee had made. But, because you don't want them to feel that these decisions were imposed on them, you decide to give them the opportunity to vote—sure that, after a very thorough and reasoned presentation, you would get a clear majority for your decision on each vote.

Your Hidden X here is that they will feel involved in the decision and not see you as a dictator. So you choose the response technology to support this X. But what if the vote goes against you, in spite of your best arguments? There on the screen, for everyone to see, is lack of support for your decisions—exactly the opposite of your true X. You were undone by your choice of technology. It didn't enable you to reach your X; it worked against you.

As these examples show, in this new and evolving communication environment, understanding the value and function of your X is even more important. Based on what's happening in the moment, you may have to adjust your content, but in ways that still target on your X. Or as a result of immediate feedback or even a technological glitch, you may have to revise your X, a decision that will inevitably entail a revision of your content or format as well.

Technology and Your Style

As communication situations incorporate more technology, the key style issues for the individual speaker are feeling in control and connecting with your listeners. It's gotten pretty complicated: You have to focus not only on what you're saying and how you're saying it, but also on taking in all the various signals and responses coming in to you from "out there," sometimes with a second or two of delay. There may be this huge picture of yourself on a screen that magnifies every sign of nervousness. An audience in front of you and a camera transmitting you to other audiences elsewhere. Perhaps a "floor man," a studio director, a TelePromp-Ter. And always the threat of a glitch somewhere along the line. You don't feel fully in control and that's understandable. You aren't. And in spite of all this technology that literally "connects" you to more people in more immediate ways, it's hard to make and maintain what feels like a real connection.

In fact, some of my clients have recognized that this environment is just too demanding to be managed by a business executive. For the two chat room meetings I discussed, a professional broadcaster was used as the "host." This person was the center of the meeting—responsible for introducing each part and, with a microphone in one ear, getting information and direction from the studio director. (The personality of the host becomes an important part of the meeting's success; he or she must do more than coordinate all of the elements effectively; the host must provide energy and liveliness, and demonstrate some understanding of the issues involved in the meeting.)

How do you as the speaker make a real connection in such a fast, multifaceted communication situation? You start by determining who your listener is.

Who Is Your Listener?

When you have people participating in meetings in remote locations—by video conference, audio or video feed, even computer link—it's not so easy to define exactly who your listener is when it comes to reaching out and going for the connection. For many years I've coached clients for situations that involved video cameras. My consistent advice has been to talk to the people in the room and ignore the camera. Those looking at you on a screen somewhere else will sense your connection with those in the room and share it indirectly.

But now, when audiences elsewhere are participating more in the meeting or the event, the question of who your listener is has become more complicated. In fact, I've come to the point of modifying my advice. If the listeners at a remote location are just as important to the accomplishment of your X as those who are physically in front of you, then you've got to reach out to them, too. The easiest way is to spend more time during your talk looking in the direction of the camera, which is usually at the back of the room. Treat the camera as an individual audience member. Work to connect with the audience near the camera, and come back more frequently to the camera itself.

But there are some problems with this approach, too. If your on-site audience is large, they'll need more energy from you; you'll have to work harder for the connection. But your remote audiences are seeing and hearing you through the medium of television, whose magic is in the intimacy and directness of the close-up and the way it creates a personal, conversational feeling. I'm sure you're seeing the problem. If you concentrate on the elements of delivery that will work better for the large audience in front of you, you're likely to come across as exaggerated or trying too hard to your remote audiences. Perhaps not even "real."

I have no easy answer for this dilemma, except to put it on the table. It's an area of choice, and sometimes it will be a hard one. But no matter what you choose, you're likely to be effective if you reach out to *someone* in as natural and relaxed a way as possible. As long as you're making a genuine connection with some listeners, the others will notice it and share it to some degree.

Energy can also be an issue—not necessarily for you as the speaker but for listeners who are physically distant from you. I have been both in the studio audience for a broadcast meeting and at a remote site, and I can tell you that there is more energy at the broadcast site. I felt more involved, more present. I paid more attention. As a speaker, you have to work to use your own energy to "pull in" those people so far away. In a videoconference meeting, where more than one person is participating at any location, it's important that you use the camera controls to zoom in when someone is speaking, go wide when there is active and quick discussion, or pan the room. It makes a big difference for anyone participating at another location—and especially if that person, as is sometimes my case, is more of an observer making occasional comments. The camera movements tend to duplicate what your own eyes would be doing if you were actually in the room. They keep your energy up and help you feel involved. This takes more attention from someone at the main location; but it pays off in results. And not just because it keeps people more awake. It sends the message that they know you're out there and want you involved. It's part of making the connection.

It's clear that technology, which has become pervasive in all our lives, is transforming the way businesspeople communicate—and giving them more choices. That means, of course, more demands to choose the appropriate medium and to use it effectively. Though all this may seem rather daunting, I'm actually excited about the uses of new technology in communication because the things it demands of a speaker to be effective are, in fact, what I've been advocating for years: a clear X; authority; energy; awareness; connection. The technology is actually forcing speakers, and companies, to confront these issues more directly than ever. And the pressure will only increase. We can be sure that technology will continue to change and offer us ever-newer ways of communicating within groups and across distances. The trend toward more participation and interactivity will certainly accelerate as a younger generation, more comfortable with technology, moves into positions of authority in companies. But the basic principles of communication will remain the same: the primacy of the individual speaker, in control of herself and connecting with others;

and the paramount importance of focus—of determining your X and aligning all the resources of the communication situation, personal and technological, toward accomplishing it. If you keep a firm hold on these principles, you can make effective use of any innovation in communication technology.

CHAPTER THIRTEEN

The Manuscript Speech

Most business presentations don't require fully written speeches. Speaking from an outline will work in most situations, and it's more alive than reading from a written document. The outline serves as a road map for what you want to say in the time you've got. Not only do you have the right to an outline or notes for your talk when you get up to speak; to do otherwise shows a lack of preparation. So don't be defensive about having notes or try to hide them from your audience.

The number and extent of your notes will depend on your familiarity with the material, but they probably should contain at least your Opening and your Close, your Message, and the main questions and answers raised by your Message. You may also want notes to remind you where to use visual aids or some other resource. And it's a good idea to indicate on your notes how much time you've given yourself for each point.

The form in which you keep your notes is up to you; use what works best. Some people prefer legal pads, others small index cards they can keep in an inside pocket until they're ready to speak. Whatever you prefer, I'd recommend that you find a place to put your notes down so that you don't have to carry them or keep putting them in or taking them out of your pocket, drawing attention to them unnecessarily. You don't need, and probably won't have, a lectern for most informal talks and presentations, but it's perfectly acceptable to keep your notes on a nearby table, for example. All you need is a place to put them where you can check them easily when necessary.

One last but very important point about using notes: When you check your notes, take a comfortable pause and break contact with your listeners. Don't rush it or look furtive, as if there's something wrong with having notes. You will demonstrate authority to your listeners when you take the time you need to remind yourself of your next point.

Sometimes a Manuscript Makes Sense

There are situations when speaking from a complete text or manuscript makes sense. If a speech is to be recorded or printed, for example, many more people may hear portions of it on radio or television or read it in a newspaper, a journal, or on-line than will hear it delivered by you live. Also, large companies may have half a dozen or so top executives simultaneously delivering identical speeches on important areas of company policy to various audiences around the world, and for the sake of consistency each speaker must deliver the same message.

Then, too, a script is usually the best way of ensuring that speeches being translated into a foreign language are not misinterpreted because of slang, industry jargon, or figures of speech. You may go the manuscript route because of legal issues (where the exact wording is critical). And, finally, there are those talks that many senior executives get invited to give to a variety of audiences on topics that require a researcher or a writer to prepare for them.

If you're in one of these situations, and have decided to use a manuscript speech, you have one major challenge: How do you turn an inanimate product—a manuscript—into the dynamic, living process that is speaking? To give life to any speaking situation, you must connect and interact with the audience. The manuscript is a barrier to that interaction and endangers the basic qualities of an effective spoken image. If you read a speech, you lose authority; if your energy goes down to the lectern instead of out to the audience, you seem to lack commitment; and it is difficult to have audience awareness if you're not looking at them. If you can't do without a manuscript, your goal should be to retain authority, energy, and audience awareness by using a delivery that is as extemporaneous and alive as you can make it.

A manuscript speech must be written and edited for speaking, and then thoroughly rehearsed. Don't make the mistake of thinking that because you have every word of your talk in front of you that the tasks of preparation and rehearsal will be easier. In fact, it takes more work to prepare and deliver an effective manuscript speech than one from notes or an outline. Let's look at the process.

Preparing the Manuscript

Let's suppose that you're working with a speechwriter (but you can apply the same principles to preparing your own manuscript). Many executives think about the overall topic or the occasion first and what they want to say second. So you might say to a speechwriter, "I'm speaking to the Commonwealth Club about interest rates and economic growth. Bring me a thirty-minute speech." The speechwriter scurries off and comes back a few days later with a bundle of pages that you look at, only to conclude, "This won't do; it's not what I wanted to say."

As you have seen before in this book, you don't get the results you want without devoting time and thought to your Point X and the Message you want to deliver. You can't say what you want to say by giving up your responsibility for your content to another person. If the writer doesn't push hard enough for direction, it's your responsibility to provide it. A good speechwriter or collaborator can help you develop a Message, or even suggest some possibilities. But you have to provide the target—Point X—for the Message, as well as indicate areas you want or need to cover.

Once you've discussed with the writer what you want to say and the main ideas you think should go into the speech, your next step is to ask the writer for an outline, not a complete text. This allows you to make necessary changes early in the process—before hours are spent preparing a document that will have to be done over from scratch if it's not right. Moreover, a speech written without your input is likely to have none of the personal flavor you would put into it; you might as well be what television people call a "talking head." This is not a complimentary term; it describes a person who doesn't know what he's talking about. Once you know what you want to talk about and have it outlined to your satisfaction, the writer can do the time-consuming job of research and fitting the pieces together.

I've found that one of the best ways to put live, spoken language into a manuscript speech is to actually talk it through. When you have your outline, fleshed out with supporting details by the speechwriter or researcher, sit down with a tape recorder and, from that outline, talk over each main idea within the time you've allowed yourself for it. If, for example, you've allowed yourself five minutes for the first answer to the question your Message raises, talk it through for five minutes. Then play it back to see how it sounds. When it sounds pretty good to you, go on to the next answer, and so on through the speech. Then have the tape transcribed. With editing, this transcription should give you the final version of your speech, and it's done with the dynamic spoken word—your own spoken words, at that—and not written language more appropriate for an article meant to be read, not heard.

Editing the Manuscript

If you've used the tape recorder method, the manuscript probably won't need as much editing as one that was written from the beginning. But when you look at the transcription, be careful not to put the written word back in. Don't eliminate contractions. Don't lengthen sentences or do anything else that will make the language more formal or stilted.

If you're working with a manuscript that began as a written document, your goal is to make the written words into effective spoken words. Here are some tips for editing:

- Use short, direct sentences, because that's the way most people talk. If a sentence is more than two lines on a page, it's too long for you to say comfortably and probably too long to have much impact on your listeners.
- Use simple, direct language. Don't try to impress your listeners with your vocabulary. They'll think you're boring at best or pedantic at worst. Language that gets right to the point is best.
- Use contractions. You use them in daily conversation, so why not use them when you speak to an audience? They're among the natural mannerisms that bring you down to earth as a speaker and make you real and human to an audience.
- After you've done the first two steps, mark your script where you will pause. This is a better system than underlining for

emphasis. People talk in gushes of words, in phrases that have rhythm and flow. Reading can kill the natural rhythm of conversation. Read the edited script out loud, and listen for the places where you would naturally pause to take a breath or complete a unit of thought. Then make a vertical line in the text every place where you paused. This will keep the conversational rhythm, and if the pause is in the right place, the emphasis will be in the right place. You'll also breathe in the right places, so you won't be gasping for air at the end of each sentence.

An effective way of editing your manuscript and marking it for pauses is shown in the following example. Note that single slashes are used for pauses and double slashes for the ends of sentences.

~~THANK YOU, MR. BROWN, AND~~ GOOD MORNING, ~~LADIES AND GENTLEMEN~~ . . . FELLOW EDUCATORS . . . FELLOW **AND**

MARKETERS //~~IT'S A DISTINCT PLEASURE TO BE WITH YOU TODAY.~~

'S **THOSE**

IT ~~IS~~ NO ACCIDENT THAT I JUST USED ~~TWO~~ TERMS ~~EDUCATORS AND MARKETERS~~ TO DESCRIBE US //. ~~YOU AND ME.~~ THE REASON THAT I CHOSE ~~TO RELATE~~ THEM, / ~~QUITE SIMPLY,~~ IS THAT ~~THE~~ INSTITUTIONS ~~YOU REPRESENT~~ AND **YOUR** COMPANIES LIKE MINE / REALLY HAVE A ~~GREAT DEAL~~ IN **LOT** COMMON //

WE IN THE ABC COMPANY ARE PRIMARILY MARKETERS, / BUT ~~HAVE~~ A MAJOR ROLE/ AS EDUCATORS IN THE LIVES OF **PLAY** THOUSANDS OF OUR EMPLOYEES// ON THE OTHER HAND, YOU

'RE
~~ARE~~ PRIMARILY EDUCATORS, / BUT ~~HAVE~~ **PLAY** A UNIQUE ROLE ~~TO~~

WE HAVE A
~~PLAY~~ AS MARKETERS OF YOUR PRODUCTS. // ~~NOW, IF WE CAN~~
LOT TO LEARN FROM EACH OTHER / THAT
~~UNDERSTAND EACH OTHER IN THIS CONTEXT, WE CAN REAP~~
COULD HELP BOTH OF US / NOT ONLY
~~CONSIDERABLE MUTUAL BENEFIT, NOT ONLY DURING THIS~~
NOW / BUT FOR MANY YEARS TO
~~MORNING, OR DURING THE YEARS OF THE COMING DECADE,~~
COME //
~~BUT ALSO FOR MANY YEARS TO COME.~~

GOOD MORNING, FELLOW EDUCATORS AND FELLOW MARKETERS //

IT'S NO ACCIDENT THAT I JUST USED THOSE TERMS TO DESCRIBE US // THE REASON THAT I CHOSE THEM / IS THAT YOUR INSTITUTIONS AND COMPANIES LIKE MINE / REALLY HAVE A LOT IN COMMON //

WE IN THE ABC COMPANY ARE PRIMARILY MARKETERS / BUT PLAY A MAJOR ROLE/ AS EDUCATORS IN THE LIVES OF THOUSANDS OF OUR EMPLOYEES // ON THE OTHER HAND, YOU'RE PRIMARILY EDUCATORS / BUT PLAY A UNIQUE ROLE AS MARKETERS OF YOUR PRODUCTS // WE HAVE A LOT TO LEARN FROM EACH OTHER/ THAT COULD HELP BOTH OF US / NOT ONLY NOW / BUT FOR MANY YEARS TO COME//

The goal of the editing is to make your manuscript as natural and conversational as possible. It should make the inanimate manuscript come alive with spoken language. It follows that the only way you can edit it effectively is to talk it out loud. Not silently. You can even whisper it, but you have to feel and hear the rhythm of the words.

Delivering the Manuscript Speech

You now have an effective "speaking" text. But you'll have to practice if you are to do more than just stand up and read to your audience. The audience will know if you've rehearsed or not. If you keep your head buried in the speech, stumble over your words, or make little or no connection with your listeners, you clearly have not devoted enough time to rehearsal. A manuscript speech is no different from an extemporaneous one: It should sound as if it's coming from your gut at the moment of delivery.

Practice until you have a firm grasp of what you want to say and how to say it. It's the same kind of preparation you'd put into any other business situation, or into learning a sport, for that matter. Practice is something the naturals do without prompting. You may feel reluctant or embarrassed to rehearse in front of your colleagues; but if you don't, you'll do your experimenting at the wrong time—in front of your audience.

Rehearsing doesn't mean you should memorize your speech, because at that point you'll stop thinking about what you're saying and think instead about what comes next. The minute that happens, your delivery goes flat and the audience can tell the difference. Thinking about what you're saying keeps your voice and delivery full of energy. An extemporaneous speaker doesn't have this problem; she must think all the time about what she's saying. Speaking from a manuscript requires more effort here, because the temptation is ever present to slip into the role of "reader." One way speakers have of making a manuscript speech come alive is to add impromptu comments as they go along.

Without adequate rehearsal the main problem speakers have in delivering manuscript speeches is losing visual contact with their listeners. Many speakers try to remedy this by simply looking up and down a lot as they read. Not only does this not provide real connection, but half their content is being delivered down to the lectern. I recommend that speakers look down and silently read to a pause mark, then look up and speak the phrase focusing fully on a single listener. Then look down, pick up the next phrase, then deliver it to another listener.

This "read to self, talk to listener" process may sound artificial, and even slow, but if you've practiced enough, you will be familiar with the text; a quick glance at the page is all you'll need to take in the next phrase, and you'll actually find yourself needing fewer of those downward glances than you thought. Seeing your listener even when you "read" gives you a much more energetic, committed delivery.

Turning pages can be distracting both for you and for your listeners. Many people prefer to slide pages to one side as they finish them, which has the added benefit of letting the speaker follow the words from the bottom of one page to the top of the next. There's a device on the market called a speech box; you can carry your speech in it and also slide pages into it as you're finished reading them. If you must use loose pages, make sure they're numbered in case you drop them and wind up literally groping for words.

Speech Prompters

Often, especially for large audiences, the manuscript speech is put on a speech prompter. Instead of pages of the script in front of you on the lectern, your text appears on a prompter. There are two kinds of speech prompters. The first is the plastic lectern that gives you a reflected view of a large-print manuscript as you speak to the audience. The second is the TelePrompTer, a device that runs the manuscript, again in large type, across the lens of a camera as the speaker reads for television. The audience is supposedly unaware of the prompter in each case. While TelePrompTers were originally used solely in television studios, they are common now at large business meetings where video cameras and screens make live speakers larger and more real to audiences in conventional-style auditoriums.

A prompter of either kind can be useful to you, but don't make the mistake of thinking it can take the place of rehearsal or that it can replace really seeing your listeners.

The plastic lectern prompter is used in pairs, in front of the speaker on each side. The manuscript, which rolls from bottom to top as you read, is invisible to the audience. The prompter thus lets you look up toward your audience giving the impression of eye contact while actually reading off the prompter. But as you know from the style section of this book, the audience can tell when someone is really trying to connect with them. Simply moving your head from side to side as you look from one prompter to another may give the illusion of contact, but will give you none of the benefits of real audience awareness. You'll sound flat and look flat, and the audience won't feel spoken to.

Speech prompters and video screens are becoming more a part of business life as meetings get larger and use more complicated audiovisual support and technology. Their increasing use points to the need for more rehearsal time rather than less, because the person rolling the manuscript through the prompter needs to become familiar with your pace.

Recently the president of a major corporation was announcing a new advertising campaign to an audience of 3,000 to 4,000 people. His close-up image was being projected on a large video screen behind him, and a TelePrompTer in front of the camera lens contained his notes. He had rehearsed and was well prepared, so he was able to reach out and connect with his audience. I felt that his reaching out was due more to practice and preparation than to the prompter, because his projected image would have revealed any nervousness or discomfort in his delivery.

On one occasion I watched an executive use a prompter to deliver a speech he had given several times before. His previous experiences with the talk apparently made him overconfident, and he left his manuscript backstage. He had placed all his trust in the technology, and halfway through his speech the prompter broke down. He was unable to fake it for more than a few minutes, and someone finally had to run backstage for his script. It's one thing to have technology support you, but this was a graphic demonstration of the need to recognize its limits: There is no substitute for thorough preparation, rehearsal, and attention to detail.

So, to sum up: There are occasions when a manuscript speech, rather than notes or an outline, makes sense for a speaker. But a manuscript can be a barrier to the interaction that makes things happen between a speaker and an audience. To overcome this barrier takes commitment and time—first to develop a manuscript that "talks," and then to deliver it in a way that feels fresh and real to your listeners.

CHAPTER FOURTEEN

Television and the Media Interview

For many years businesspeople approached the media defensively. The "investigative reporting" popular with both national and local media tended to create an adversarial attitude toward the subject of an interview or a story, and consequently most businesspeople tried to avoid media encounters. If they worked to improve their skills in interviews, it was to avoid embarrassment on camera or in print.

The mechanics of television, in particular, only added to their discomfort. Like large, heavily produced meetings, television makes us feel less in control than situations not so thoroughly dictated by technology. When we're not in control, we feel we can't be as effective.

The defensive attitude toward the media still exists in the business community today, and not without reason. But things have changed, too. Business is news in a way it hasn't been before. There is a sense that what happens in the world economy often has more importance than what happens in Washington. Combining with this greater, and generally more positive, interest in business is the huge increase in demand for content as a result of the growth of media distribution channels. The result is opportunity.

Now you as a businessperson can take advantage of the media to help you reach your key constituencies in the business community and the community at large. You have the opportunity to use the media to get your message out. To promote your company's interests and goals. To influence government policy. To shape investor attitudes. To create consumer interest.

So being effective in dealing with the media today can mean a lot more for you than simply avoiding embarrassment. It can impact your bottom line in positive ways. More than ever before, it's worth the time and effort to get comfortable with the media, and especially with television.

Television

We tend to think we have to be different for TV. Accustomed as we are to seeing other people's warts exposed on the screen, we think television requires us to be perfect. Perfection is not only an intimidating goal; it's an impossible one.

What scares people the most about video, however, is the same thing that provides the medium with its unique, special magic: the intimacy of the close-up. The camera zooms in for a close shot, and suddenly we see people in a way we never see them in real life. When you look at a full-face shot of a newscaster or of a businessperson being interviewed, you see that person as close as if the two of you were kissing. When you watch yourself in a shot like that, you see things about yourself that you don't normally see: "That freckle on my nose . . . was it there this morning when I was brushing my teeth?" And those questions can grow naturally into fears: "Is my hair really that thin? Do I look that pale?" Unlike the mirror you gaze into as you brush your teeth and comb your hair, the camera is an unbiased, objective, unblinking viewer. It doesn't allow us the view of reality that we prefer.

But if the close-up isn't used, television isn't nearly as interesting; the intimacy of a single, animated face is what makes video such a wonderful medium. It brings us much closer to the person and makes us feel as if we're seeing more of him. That's what makes us want to watch it.

What does this all mean for the businessman or businesswoman who must deal with this wonderful, terrifying medium? Throughout this book you've learned that effective speaking is a matter of making choices that work for you and project the best of what you are. You have to know what you want to happen and focus on conveying your message and connecting with your audience.

The rules for television effectiveness are the same as for any other speaking situation. People who apply their own energy, demonstrate an awareness of the audience, and are prepared to say what they have to say with authority can communicate as well on television as any media professional.

Getting Familiar with Television

When you know you're going to be on television, whether you'll be talking to an interviewer or just to a camera (as in a taped message to colleagues or employees), you should take time to familiarize yourself with the mechanics of the medium. Local TV stations offer tours that show visitors the whole process. Many of them will probably do this for you privately and even let you sit in the back of the studio while the local news is being aired.

No matter how you choose to go about it, you should treat this familiarization with the TV studio as part of your job. It's as basic as locating hand and foot controls and learning traffic signals before you drive. If you approach it as a job-related project, you'll quickly learn that an appearance on television is not a trip into the mysterious unknown.

The action in a TV studio takes place in a small circle of light. This is the set, or the area where the interview is being conducted. Activities outside the circle of light, while they may be interesting and will certainly be distracting, should not concern you. People will be dragging cables, moving cameras, even talking to one another. The set itself will be distracting: the expensive-looking anchor desk you see on the screen is hammered together out of plywood and the plush carpet that looks so luxurious on the air is usually unbound, ragged at the edges, and dotted with cigarette burns and wads of chewing gum. It's good for you to notice all this, because it helps keep the medium of television in perspective.

When a camera crew comes to your office for an interview, the mechanics are much the same. There's no question it's hard to concentrate when even one or two uninterested strangers (the technicians) are standing around listening to you and an interviewer talk. But television has to carry a lot of baggage around with it. While you're being interviewed, light stands seem to teeter in every corner of your office, threatening to fall or be kicked over onto your potted plants. The camera tripod digs into your carpet. Cables are everywhere. Sometimes the bright TV lights will blow the fuses in your office. The camera operator will shove his way behind your desk to get a reverse, or cutaway, shot of the interviewer; the lighting technician will leaf through the books in your bookshelf; the sound man may yawn a lot. No wonder you're distracted!

Once you've seen all this, forget it. All that matters is the way you relate to the interviewer. Everything else that's going on has to do with the technical requirements for getting this brief moment of television on the air. This is somebody else's concern, and you don't need to worry about it. Concentrate on delivering your message.

"Where Do I Look?"

When you're being interviewed, the message you're delivering is to the interviewer. When you're alone with the camera, your message is to the people who will view you through its lens. Almost all your media appearances will involve exchanges with one or more other people, as in a panel discussion. Focus your attention on the people who are there, to whom you are talking. Don't worry about the camera. That's the job of the production crew. Even though you know that from a business standpoint you are there to sell your point of view to the audience at home, you do that best by coming across in a committed, sensitive way to the people in the studio. The only way you can show your commitment and sensitivity is to the live human beings who are there interacting with you and with whom you must establish rapport. If you get an exciting exchange going with the interviewer, the feeling of excitement is passed on to the viewer.

Nothing can make you look more foolish than a shot that finds you looking at the wrong camera. It looks to the audience as if you're ignoring the human beings there with you and talking to the air. Don't try to beat the professionals at their own game. It's just too dangerous for a television amateur—which is what most businesspeople are no matter how much time they spend being interviewed—to try to outguess the camera by following the little red monitor light around.

As a former television interviewer, I can say that what always made an interview interesting was the direct interaction between the people talking. This was just as true in a friendly interview as in one where I was more aggressive. And as an interviewee, I have found that the more I focus on establishing a relationship and conveying my message to the questioner, not to the camera, the more effective I am.

When there is no interviewer or no panel members, as when you are making a promotional tape, delivering remarks welcoming people to a convention or meeting you can't attend, or doing a training tape of some kind, the only thing you can do is to talk to the camera.

Some people say you have to fall in love with the camera. That's not an easy image for businesspeople to relate to, and I'm not so sure it's accurate, anyway. What you can do instead is replace the camera in your mind's eye with one person, someone likely to be in your audience. Envision your viewer as you talk to the camera; it's a good way to forget you're talking to a machine.

When I was the host of a children's show on network television in Canada, I opened the show by talking directly to the camera. I found it helped to visualize a young niece of mine, and every word that I said was to her. By talking to that child, I think I came across in a direct and intimate way to the children who were watching. A local television anchorman once told me that he tried to envision a gray-haired grandmother, rocking and knitting, with a cat in her lap. And the host of a public affairs talk show says that when she talks to the camera, she tries to see a crusty former governor on the other side of the lens.

When I prepare tapes for workshops at Speakeasy that I can't attend, I find a subtle difference in tone when I haven't spent enough time visualizing the audience in my mind. Without being able to see whom I'm talking to, I feel a slight lack of the energy and awareness that make my connection with the audience more real, and my message is less effective. Remember your audience analysis. Since you've learned something about your listeners in planning your content, you should have a picture of them and reflect that awareness in your style.

None of this means that you have to be an actor to be effective when you talk to the camera. You are only placing yourself in a real situation as much as you can by visualizing one person to talk to instead of a machine. Imagining that you are talking to someone also makes it easier to forget the strangers in the room.

Conveying Authority on Television

By now, everybody knows television is not a miracle medium whose best practitioners are all perfect. Knowing that being effective doesn't mean being perfect is the first step toward being in control, which is in turn the first step in projecting authority.

Acknowledging the presence of TV's technological requirements and the occasional problems they create is one effective cure for the feeling that you have to be perfect for television. If you flub a line in real life, in a personal conversation, or in a speech or presentation, you don't have the chance to go back, erase it, and start over. In an interview, you would correct a mistake after the fact just as you would in any conversation. When you're making a videotape, there's nothing to prohibit letting a minor human error stand alongside your correction.

I saw one chief executive muff a line during a videotaping session for which he'd had little time to rehearse. Instead of halting the proceedings to correct his error, he shrugged, smiled, and said to the camera, "Well, that's what happens when they give you these things to read at the last minute." It was really the moment when his speech came alive. He said, in effect, "Hey, I'm not perfect." And he admitted what everybody watching would know anyway—he was in a situation dictated by technological circumstances. But instead of being the victim of those circumstances, he took control and established his authority. He went ahead with his message, as if to say the mechanics were not important enough to make him interrupt what he was giving to his audience.

It takes a strong, confident speaker to make that kind of admission. But one who does it relates better to the audience because she strips away the mechanical barriers that separate them. You gain control and show authority on television as you do in any speaking situation, but you should also seek a comfortable relationship with its mechanical aspects to assure they won't interfere with communication between you and your audience.

Two Tips for Television

No discussion of television would be complete without mentioning the requirements of dressing for the camera and moving in a way that lets you express energy and be comfortable without being distracting.

If you watch much television, you probably have a pretty good idea of what kinds of clothes work best. Solid colors and muted stripes are better than busy patterns. Avoid shiny fabrics that can reflect the glare of the lights. You're generally better off avoiding black, white, and red and sticking to the blues, grays, and beiges of conventional business attire. Keep your hairstyle simple. Wear a minimum of jewelry, especially the dangly, jangly kind that might make noise, catch the lights, or otherwise draw attention to itself.

A balanced, settled posture is the best base from which to speak for television, as it is for other speaking situations. Any movement should try to convey a Message. People seated for a television interview often release their nervousness by swiveling furiously in their chairs. This or any other motion that doesn't stem directly from the expression of your Message can be extremely distracting on camera. Sit quietly when you are not speaking.

The Media Interview

You won't have to struggle to draw out questions during encounters with the media. Just as in any presentation, to make something happen in an interview with a television, radio, or newspaper reporter, you have to be certain of your Point X. What happens isn't totally up to the reporter, and what you want to happen can determine how you choose to answer certain questions. So your approach to a media encounter should start with organizing your content according to your analysis of the situation and audience.

Nor is a media encounter different from any other speaking situation: You need to be prepared. Rehearsal, in which you have someone ask you the tough questions, then becomes a must. Don't rehearse with the idea of memorizing the answers to all the questions you anticipate. Rehearse to get comfortable with the really tough questions that may bring out your Hidden X's. No matter how well you think you know the answers, the subject, and your Hidden X's, until someone really presses you, you won't know what you're comfortable with and what you're not.

I was preparing an executive for a stockholders' meeting that was to be covered by the media and at which a major stockholder was expected to mount a takeover bid. Every time the executive was asked about the takeover bid, he gave a weak, wishy-washy answer. At the end of the rehearsal session the executive wanted to know how his style had been. "Your style was fine," I answered. "The question is, what was your answer on the subject of a takeover? You've been waffling, and right now you don't know what you want to happen. Before you go into that meeting, you have to make a fundamental decision about what you want to happen, and neither your public relations people nor I can do that for you." Rehearsal forces you to come to grips with where you are with the content. Dealing with the hard questions beforehand also can help you arrive at substantive answers. If you don't beat around the bush during an interview, you'll be more likely to avoid escalating an encounter into a confrontation.

The lessons contained in the style section of this book will help you avoid confrontations; authority and energy give your answers the credibility they deserve; and audience awareness keeps you from antagonizing reporters.

Questions: How Do You Answer Them?

You usually don't have much choice about what questions reporters ask or how they ask them, but you do have a choice about the way you answer them. No one can take that choice away from you. Here are some things to think about as you prepare for a tough media interview (or a Q&A session).

1. How do you want to come across? This is the area of Hidden X's. Most people in business and public service want to come across as open and knowledgeable. You may have other or additional Hidden X's of your own for a particular Q&A or interview situation. Whatever they are, your answers are likely to be better if you've taken some time before the interview to examine them. Wanting to be open and knowledgeable, for example, is usually OK, but even this Hidden X can get you in trouble.

Being open: There may be times when you're not at liberty to speak or when it's not appropriate for you to be the one answering even if you do know the answer.

Being knowledgeable: This Hidden X will always tempt you to give too much information, too many details, too much background. It can also be troublesome in situations when you really don't know the answer. How comfortable are you with acknowledging that you don't know?

2. What do you want to get across? There will be many Q&A situations where you'll have a Message you want to get across

about your company's position or your department's needs. The interview is an opportunity for you to get that Message across. So in addition to taking time beforehand to examine your Hidden X's, take time to select your Point X for the interview. Also try developing some sample Messages that would target on that X. You'll usually find that many of the questions you're asked will give you the opportunity to send out your Messages, either directly or by the technique known as bridging. If you've done this kind of homework, you'll go into the interview in a proactive rather than reactive frame of mind.

There are questions—and there are questions. Your questioner has a right to have his or her question listened to and acknowledged—but the questioner (in most situations) does not have the right to a particular answer. Whether and how you answer a question is your choice. You are likely to make a more effective choice if you are familiar with the types of questions people generally ask.

Type A: "Journalist's questions." These are the straightforward, information-oriented questions you can usually anticipate and prepare rough answers for.

Who (is responsible? was involved?)
What (do you do? happened? are you doing about it?)
Why (did it happen? are you doing it this way?)
When (did it happen? did you find out about it? will the report be out? will the decision be reached?)
How (did it happen? are you dealing with it?)

Type B: Questions that tend to put you on the spot. You will often want to renegotiate these questions before you answer them.

The *yes-or-no question:* An invitation to oversimplify.
The *A-or-B question:* A close relative of the yes-or-no.
The *false-premise or loaded question:* Opens with a statement that is a distortion of the facts or a misrepresentation of the

situation, of your policy, of someone else's position; or may just state a conclusion you're not ready to endorse.

The *hypothetical question:* Be very careful about answering this type of question; the real world is hard enough to deal with without having to deal with supposed situations.

These two types of questions are not always very distinct; the false-premise question, for example, will often be asked as a "journalist's question." The key is to listen for loaded words—verbs like "admit," "justify," "excuse," or phrases like "a lot of people say . . . ," "there are reports that . . . ," "why are so many . . . ?" You will usually want to renegotiate these questions by politely but firmly challenging the loaded term before you proceed to answer them.

Here is a three-step format for answering questions:

Step 1: Listen to the question. This sounds obvious, but a lot of people, especially when they're under pressure and nervous, start thinking about answers before the questioner has finished with the question. You've got to listen carefully so that you can be sure exactly what question was asked (and how it was asked).

Step 2: Pause. You don't have to answer immediately. Take a second or two to breathe and gather your thoughts. *You have that right,* and it won't come across as hesitant so long as you keep your focus on the questioner. And remember: Your pause will seem a lot longer to you than it will to your listeners.

Step 3: Answer the question. No matter how much you say, only about twenty seconds (eighty-plus words) of it is likely to show up after it's been edited for radio or TV news. Even if you're not answering for the media and don't have to worry about being edited, it's important to remember that the first part of your answer will get the most attention from your listeners. So practice answering in this order.

a. A one-sentence answer (the main point you want to make in response to the question) or a one-sentence renegotiation of the question followed by a one-sentence answer/point.

b. Two sentences of elaboration (optional).

c. An example or illustration or a follow-up promise (optional).

Examples:

• The question directly sets up one of your Messages: "How do you know your rides are safe?"

"We know our rides are safe because we inspect them every day. Safety is our number-one priority. Starting at five o'clock each morning, our crew inspects every ride in the park, and in addition, the rides are checked again on a spot basis throughout the day."

• *Bridging* from the interviewer's question to one of your Messages: "What went wrong with the safety procedures at the New Jersey theme park?"

"I really can't talk about the New Jersey park because, first, each park is separately owned and operated and, second, the ride that caused the injuries in New Jersey is one we don't have in our park. But I can talk about our outstanding safety record, which is the envy of the industry. We've never had a ride-related fatality in over a quarter of a *billion* rides that people have taken in our park."

Two don'ts for answering questions. You can choose how and whether you answer a question. But there are two choices you ought always to avoid:

1. *Don't lie*. This "don't" includes statements that while not downright untruths are nevertheless designed to mislead the listener or to create a false impression.

2. *Don't evade*. Don't answer a question that wasn't asked and expect your listeners not to know the difference. You can,

however, bridge or transition from a question you can't or don't want to answer to make a point that isn't in direct response to the question asked. Be careful, however, not to overdo this technique. If you do, you'll begin to come across like the stereotypical slick politician.

Keeping Media Encounters from Becoming Confrontations

Media encounters become confrontations because when somebody pushes, the natural reaction is to push back. The pushing starts when we give wishy-washy answers to a reporter's questions, when we don't exhibit the authority, energy, and audience awareness of an effective spoken image, and when we don't know what we want to say. Reporters and interviewers, like most of us, meet resistance with resistance.

Executives are used to being in charge. But when the tables are turned and the control is elsewhere, powerful executives often see themselves in a win-lose situation and their first reaction is to try to regain control. The results are often the opposite of what they want.

Speakeasy worked with one industrial company that sought advice on media confrontation. The company wanted to counter a well-publicized series of government charges that it had failed to comply with environmental regulations. In the "aggressive reporter versus stonewalling executive" role-playing that is a feature of many media confrontation courses, I played the reporter firing hard questions at the company president. I would bark a question into the hand-held mike and then shove it under the president's nose, then yank it back again to ask another question before he had a chance to answer. He became enraged. He just couldn't believe he was not going to have control over the microphone. This typical situation is remarkably frustrating for anyone who is used to dominating his surroundings, and that's why media interviews can be so difficult for top executives.

Executives involved in provocative media encounters should realize that they can control their content but not the mechanics of the situation.

I have seen some practiced politicians, who know when the camera is probably on a head-and-shoulders shot in a stand-up interview, gently grasp the microphone and hold on to it while they're giving their answer. They usually got away with it because they looked almost like commentators themselves. But instead of fighting for physical control of the microphone, it's better to say, "I'd like to answer your questions if you'd just give me the chance." Such an answer, combined with a low tension level and relaxed voice tone, can avoid heightening the atmosphere of confrontation. It certainly serves to point out the reporter's unfairness in not allowing the person being interviewed to answer.

When you're pushed, pushing back is rarely your best response in a confrontation. I was working once with a political candidate who had made the usual number of mistakes and misjudgments that could be magnified in the heat of the campaign. A debate among several candidates was coming up, and the man with whom I was working wanted to rehearse his responses to questions. He was concerned that his answers to reporters not give these mistakes more than the minor status they deserved. I asked him some straight but tough questions. He was direct with his answers and felt satisfied with his performance. But as we kept going, I began asking questions in a harder, pushy way. As my questions got more and more aggressive, his answers, too, became hostile and aggressive. The more I pushed, the more he came across like someone who had something to hide.

The same techniques that reduce resistance in other speaking situations apply in media encounters. I was once interviewed by a TV reporter who was hyped up and totally self-absorbed before the live interview. On the set she threw me a question and immediately looked down at her script. Then she busied herself with some quick primping before the camera came back to her. My immediate reaction was to rush into what I had to say and get it on the record quickly, but I decided instead to exhale, slow down, and talk to the reporter. I made up my mind that I could set the atmosphere, and as I continued to talk to her, she turned toward me and became more attentive. Once she focused on me, the interview went much better. It's preferable to get out less information—information that works—than to spout out everything you want to say in an atmosphere that doesn't allow you to be effective.

If you don't know the answer to a question, don't be afraid to say so. A simple "I don't know" is better than a nonanswer, in which your lack of knowledge becomes clear in any case. Admitting that you don't know can also save you from creating new questions or misunderstandings. It may be hard to confess that you don't know all the facts or details, but honesty removes the possibility that you'll give misleading or wrong information. And if it's all that important, as when a reporter is working on a deadline story, you can always offer to get back to her with an answer. You can even have associates pursue the information as the interview continues.

Sometimes, of course, you may not want to answer a reporter's question in an interview. Reasons for this could include pending legal action, trade secrets, and a host of other factors involving sensitive business operations. (Personnel matters, for example, usually aren't talked about publicly in most organizations.) Or you may have other good reasons for not wanting to answer a question. Your company may have its own carefully orchestrated timetable for releasing information about new board members or a new product it plans to market. Again, stating your case is usually the best way to handle this—"I can't answer because we're in court on that issue" or "I prefer not to say right now. We have a news conference scheduled on that matter in two days." These may not be the answers the reporter would like to have, but she understands them. They make it clear where you stand and why you're not giving her the real answer. This is part of the everyday world of media encounters.

Getting Your Message Out

In a media interview, as in any speaking situation, you want to make something happen, you have a Message—points you want to make and information you want to get across. But sometimes the questions don't allow you to make your points. If the line of questioning doesn't give you an opportunity to give information you think important, don't hesitate to turn the interview to your agenda. You can usually do this inoffensively by saying something like "That's an area we haven't explored, but we've developed information in another area that I think you would find interesting." This tactic will sometimes help a reporter who is struggling to get a handle on a difficult interview. And, of course, it will certainly work to your advantage, up to a point.

Delivering your own Message is a tactic to be used sparingly. If you overuse it, if you never answer the reporter's questions, it becomes quite obvious in a very short time. You exhibit a lack of audience awareness when you continue to say, in effect, "Well, I hear that, but I'm ignoring it, and I'm going to say what I want." People have every right to get irritated in such a case, and you're often better off just saying that you can't or won't answer the question. And don't make the mistake of thinking that you can avoid discussion of a sensitive area if that's what you agreed to be interviewed about.

When to Say Nothing

Don't feel compelled to fill silences. This is one of the surest ways of blurting out information that you don't want to relate. Suppose a reporter has asked you a question in an interview and you've answered it, or at least you've said as much as you want to say. But instead of asking you another question when you've finished, the reporter waits. The silence grows. It's as if he knows you've got more to say and he's waiting for you to say it. He keeps waiting. Finally, you're desperate to end the silence and out tumbles the very thing you didn't want to say. This, of course, is the one thing that will make the news, because instead of thinking about what you really want to say, you're thinking about filling that awkward silence.

This happened in a television interview with the head of Atlanta's convention bureau at a time several years ago when the city was suffering image problems—and a potential loss of convention business—because of the widely publicized murder of a conventioneer. The executive felt he'd handled the interview well until he saw the story on network television. The story carried only the very end of his interview, when he had become bothered by the silence and blurted out, "If there is one more murder of a conventioneer in this city, we're flat out of business." It's the reporter's job to fill the silence; let him worry about it. Push back your social instinct to keep the conversation going. Give your answer and then keep quiet until you answer the next question.

Avoid Insider's Language

I've already mentioned the importance of talking in clear, direct language that people can understand. This is good advice in any speaking situation, but it's especially important in media encounters, when the people you are actually talking to are the general public through the television screen, radio speaker, or newspaper. Remember that while you are familiar with the jargon of your industry, most people aren't. Translate for them. Speak in terms that break the code and let the public know in everyday language what your Message is. Discard the acronyms that are part of your office talk and try to think how you would like to have things described if you were an industry outsider. Clarity of language is the essence of effective communication in any situation.

Business is news today in a way it has never been before. More people are investing in the stock market, and some business leaders have attained celebrity status. Whatever business you're in, you're likely to attract the media's attention at some point or another. But I encourage you to be proactive: Make media interviews and announcements part of your business communication plan. Determine what you want to say and rehearse how you want to say it—without expecting perfection from yourself. If you do these things, you'll be able to use the media to advance your business objectives and to dramatically extend your ability to make things happen.

Conclusion

Now that you've finished this book, what have you learned? You haven't learned formulas that will guarantee effective content and style every time you make a presentation. There are no pat formulas and there are no guarantees, because each speaker is an individual and each speaking occasion is unique.

Your listeners' needs and your own needs will change from situation to situation. The reason the content-planning process I've outlined in this book will work in all your communication situations is that it won't allow you to treat them all the same. Instead, it helps you identify what is unique in each situation and use that uniqueness to get the result you want. The process asks you the same questions, but your answers keep changing.

So too with the techniques in this book for effective delivery: they are not meant to produce perfect, polished robots. All of them have the speaker as their basis—and every speaker is an individual. I strongly believe no speaker can be really effective unless he is being himself. The techniques are just ways to help each individual express the best of what he or she is. Just as the content of your presentation should take full account of the uniqueness of the occasion, so too your style should express the uniqueness of you.

No, you haven't learned rules or formulas. Instead you've learned some questions to ask, steps to follow, techniques to explore and adapt. But they all have one and the same objective: to help you get results whenever you speak. The goal is not to have the perfect stance or absolutely the best Message—it's to make something happen. I wouldn't have written this book if my years of experience with businesspeople had not convinced me that my approach to style and content can make a big difference to a speaker's effectiveness. But this same experience convinces me that all techniques are only a means to an end—to have style and content working together to reach out and connect with your audience. When you make that connection and get the results you want, then you experience the real reward of careful planning and personal risk taking. It's the exhilaration that comes not from getting it right but from *making it happen*.

ABOUT THE AUTHOR

Internationally recognized as an expert on communication, Sandy Linver is the founder of Speakeasy Inc., a communication training and consulting company with offices in Atlanta and San Francisco. Speakeasy helps leaders at all levels reach their potential through more effective communication—internally, with their colleagues, and externally, with their clients. Among Speakeasy's clients are The Coca-Cola Company, Accenture, UPS, The Home Depot, Sprint, and Microsoft. Linver is also the author of *Speakeasy* and *The Leader's Edge*.

For more information on courses and books, please contact Speakeasy Inc., 3414 Peachtree Road, NE, Suite 800, Atlanta, GA 30326; telephone: 404-261-4029; fax: 404-266-1898.